THEORY IN CRIMINOLOGY
Contemporary Views

Volume 1
SAGE RESEARCH PROGRESS SERIES IN CRIMINOLOGY

ABOUT THIS SERIES

The SAGE RESEARCH PROGRESS SERIES IN CRIMINOLOGY is intended for those professionals and students in the fields of criminology, criminal justice, and law who are interested in the nature of current research in their fields. Each volume in the series—four to six new titles will be published in each calendar year—focuses on a theme of current and enduring concern; and each volume contains a selection of previously unpublished essays . . . drawing upon presentations made at the previous year's Annual Meeting of the American Society of Criminology.

Now in its second year, the series continues with five new volumes, composed of papers presented at the 29th Annual Meeting of the American Society of Criminology held in Atlanta, Georgia on November 16-20, 1977. The volumes in this second year of publication include:

- *Violent Crime: Historical and Contemporary Issues*
  edited by James A. Inciardi and Anne E. Pottieger
- *Law and Sanctions: Theoretical Perspectives*
  edited by Marvin D. Krohn and Ronald L. Akers
- *The Evolution of Criminal Justice: A Guide for Practical Criminologists*
  edited by John P. Conrad
- *Quantitative Studies in Criminology*
  edited by Charles Wellford
- *Discretion and Control*
  edited by Margaret Evans

Previously published volumes include:

- *Theory in Criminology: Contemporary Views*
  edited by Robert F. Meier
- *Juvenile Delinquency: Little Brother Grows Up*
  edited by Theodore N. Ferdinand
- *Contemporary Corrections: Social Control and Conflict*
  edited by C. Ronald Huff
- *Criminal Justice Planning and Development*
  edited by Alvin W. Cohn

Comments and suggestions from our readers about this series are welcome.

SERIES EDITORS:

James A. Inciardi
University of Delaware

William E. Amos
U.S. Board of Parole

SAGE RESEARCH PROGRESS SERIES IN CRIMINOLOGY
VOLUME 1

THEORY in CRIMINOLOGY
Contemporary Views

Edited by
Robert F. Meier

Published in cooperation with the
AMERICAN SOCIETY of CRIMINOLOGY

SAGE Publications   Beverly Hills   London

For information address:

SAGE PUBLICATIONS, INC.
275 South Beverly Drive
Beverly Hills, California 90212

SAGE PUBLICATIONS LTD
28 Banner Street
London EC1Y 8QE

Printed in the United States of America

International Standard Book Number 0-8039-0915-2 (cloth)
International Standard Book Number 0-8039-0910-1 (paper)
Library of Congress Catalog Card No. 77-81151

SECOND PRINTING

CONTENTS

75317

To Jennifer and Chris

Robert F. Meier
University of California,
Irvine

INTRODUCTION

One of the first tasks of those charged with organizing the 28th annual meeting of the American Society of Criminology was to discuss possible themes for the convention. The theme of any national conference should be specific enough to "organize" the papers and presentations, but, at the same time, be sufficiently broad to permit a diversity of persons, viewpoints, and interests to participate. For the criminology meetings, it was decided quite early that there would be no theme; by the time of our meeting (November 1976) the bicentennial theme would have been beaten to death—much to the relief of many. Besides, we figured, the study of criminology and criminal justice encompasses a number of practitioners and academics from many disciplines, all working on divergent aspects of law-making, law-breaking, and responses to law-breaking. We felt that a formal statement of "theme" would automatically exclude some persons from the meeting and would vitiate the diversity which has characterized the Society. The papers contained in this volume, all presented at these meetings, both reflect and demonstrate this diversity, being especially selected for this purpose.

The papers presented here reflect three main endeavors or concerns, both old and new. The first is the interest that many criminologists are displaying about the history of the discipline

(Savitz, Turner, and Dickman) and the present status of different perspectives in criminology (Michalowski). The second concern is the foundation upon which criminological theories are based, particularly with respect to bodies of literature in other fields (Hippchen), the adequacies and uses of comparative information about the incidence of crime (Pepinsky), and specific data about offenders (McCord). The third concern revolves around improving the theoretical sophistication and explanatory power of criminological theories in a discussion of an often neglected dimension of criminological theories (Garofalo), and in discussions of two areas of research which are of contemporary theoretical interest and import—deterrence (Minor) and white-collar crime (Clark and Hollinger). This volume, then, is intended to show the interests of criminologists in extending previous theoretical insights, recognizing certain "facts" with which theories of crime must deal, and in improving the power of criminological theories.

CONCERN WITH HISTORY

Elsewhere, I have argued that criminological theory represents a continuity with those views and perspectives that precede them (Meier, 1976). This continuity is one of the hallmarks of any scientific endeavor: intellectual innovations— whether they deal with methodological, conceptual, statistical, or theoretical issues—attempting to build upon, react to, or challenge those which came before. In this sense, there is nothing which is absolutely or uniquely "new," but rather there are improvements on existing developments. As any discipline matures, it attempts to legitimate its existence by playing a sort of intellectual status game. The rules of this game center around the notion of respectability; and symbols of that respectability mark the discipline's progress. Let me mention just two of the more visible signs. First, the history of the discipline becomes increasingly irrelevant for modern practitioners. Surgical techniques of the Egyptian culture of some two thousand years ago are not taught in modern medical schools; the speculative (but often prophetic) conjectures of the early astronomers are no longer of any substantive interest to their modern counterparts; even Newton's physics are of less concern today given Einstein's advances. Similarly, biology has moved beyond the work of Darwin, and mathematics beyond that of Pythagoras. But, notice too, the continuing importance of Marx, Weber, and Durkheim to contemporary social thought.[1]

A second mark of intellectual progress is that as a discipline grows, there is less and less need for a number of textbooks recounting elementary knowledge in the discipline. The reason for this is rather self-evident: as the discipline matures, there is less disagreement about elementary matters and a small number of texts can adequately cover the field. That is why there is a relatively small number of texts in such fields as physics, astronomy, and medicine (the "history-droppers"), and, conversely, why there is a large number of texts in sociology, psychology, and political science.

How does criminology stand with respect to these two benchmarks of intellectual progress? Two observations can describe the present state. First, there is still enormous concern (and mounting concern if I read things correctly) with the history and current status of criminology, and, second, there are a large number of texts which offer students basic knowledge (or, rather, different interpretations of that knowledge) of the discipline. In short, there is still tremendous disagreement about the nature of criminology, where it has been, where it is going, and where it ought to go. There is even disagreement about the presumed "facts" in the discipline relating to the nature of crime, its causes and cures, its relationship with other social, economic, and political forces, and the nature and types of public policies which are suggested by specific theoretical perspectives (see Meier and Geis, 1977). I do not mean these comments to sound condemning. (Personally, I view them as rather challenging and as affording criminologists with a degree of intellectual stimulation to counteract the complacency that lingers in other disciplines which have "solved" all of this.) I view criminology as vital, not comotose, and this vitality is rooted in the diversity of viewpoints of its practitioners, and the range of topics they choose for study.

The first paper, that by Michalowski, neatly points out this diversity in summarizing major perspectives in criminology. One method which has been adopted for "making sense" of ideas and theories in criminology is that of "paradigm," or a set of assumptions about the nature of crime, criminals, and criminal justice. Michalowski shows that with more recent, "radical" notions about crime, a general questioning about the structures of criminological thought has begun, a questioning that examines the assumptions, taken-for-granted puzzles, and ideologies of criminologists in approaching their work. Such an examination necessarily involves some historical reexamination since, as Michalowski points out, the newer ideas are linked with older ones as well as events in the larger social world. By identifying larger intellectual categories for the placement of criminological theories, Michalowski sensitizes us to the interrelatedness of these theories and their origins.

One indication that criminology is maturing is the omission of biological theories of crime in Michalowski's discussion. Savitz, Turner, and Dickman, sensitive to the historical antecedents of modern criminology, address this perspective in their "case" for Gall being the founder of criminology. On the surface, the Savitz, Turner, and Dickman paper might be dismissed as historical quibbling: what does it matter now whether Lombroso or Gall was the founder of criminology? Such a reading, however, neglects the wider implications of biological theory in criminology. The importance of Lombroso to criminology, of course, lies not in his substantive contribution to the field, but the fact that he extended the excitement generated originally by Gall, and others, about the scientific study of criminality. It was Gall, however, as these authors note, who laid the groundwork for the acclaim and criticism that Lombroso received. Moreover, this simple historical fact seems to have escaped most accounts of criminology's modest beginnings. If for no other reason than setting the record straight, Savitz et al. have performed a service for the discipline.[2]

IMPLICATIONS FOR CRIMINOLOGICAL THEORY

The scientific study of crime began within a biological framework. Aided by the tremendous influence of the works of

Darwin and Wallace, the first systematic investigators of criminal behavior, as Savitz et al. show, were met by an enthusiastic and receptive professional audience (as well as a seemingly loving public) for their work. Biologically based theories have suffered many blows to their acceptance, not the least of which were charges of racism disguised as science, a political connotation of Nazi Germany, and the inability of researchers to demonstrate convincingly the adequacy of biological theories in a social world. Still, while Lombroso had his Göring, and Hooton and Sheldon their Sutherland, interest in the biological bases of human behavior has continued to the present time. In fact, in recent years, this interest has stretched to the point where serious students of sociology—traditionally one of the most anti-biological disciplines—have begun to entertain seriously the hypothesis that biological factors are not irrelevant to theories of social behavior (Eckland, 1967; van den Berghe, 1975; see also Wilson, 1975).

Leonard Hippchen argues that biological factors have been dismissed prematurely in theories of criminal behavior. This theme is one which would receive less argument today than a decade ago, but recent reviews of this literature (see, especially, Shah and Roth, 1974) have made a similar contention, and have supported this claim with empirical research. Hippchen's paper is not meant to be an exhaustive review of such factors, but does point out certain of these conditions and discusses the importance of these factors and their implications not only for criminological theory but correctional planning as well. While Hippchen's paper could probably be criticized for its unclear distinction between what is "cause" and what is "effect," the increasing attention being given biological variables as sources of criminality points to the fact that criminologists can no longer ignore such possible relationships. At the very least, with their interdisciplinary sensitivity and background, criminologists should explore other bodies of literature which may hold promise for the construction of theories of crime.

A different issue is addressed in the paper by Harold Pepinsky: the adequacy of data about crime and social control, which often serves as a basis for theory construction. Reviewing briefly the development of criminal statistics in the United States, Pepinsky then turns to a comparative analysis of record keeping about crime in America and China, showing in the process the divergent functions and potential impact of such records. Pepinsky argues that the Chinese keep crime records primarily for the purpose of establishing precedent in dealing with interpersonal conflict in extralegal contexts (much like lawyers keep records of past court decisions), while the United States and other western nations maintain such records to document fluctuations in the incidence of criminal activity. One implication of these differing purposes is to portray to the public very different images of what crime is and the manner in which it should be handled. A more interesting implication, however, is that this knowledge itself generates crime by encouraging the citizenry to rely on public rather than private means to resolve these problems, thus turning over to the state control over this behavior.

Given differing purposes for the gathering and dissemination of criminal records and statistics, of course, is directly relevent to the construction of theory. Pepinsky does not argue that the "true" rate of crime is much lower in China as a result of record keeping than in the United States (though, I think, such a claim would not be incompatible with his thesis), but he does point to the links between knowledge about crime, the means which arise to deal with this problem and the larger social order.

The theme of acquiring reliable knowledge about criminality is also one of the themes of Joan McCord's paper on generational transmission of crime patterns. While Pepinsky suggests that criminality may not be increasing in this country though we are led to believe this is the case given the information collected about crime, McCord points more dramatically to this conclusion with some data collected from 115 pairs of fathers and sons which compares their criminal biographies. McCord finds that there is some correspondence in the criminality of each generation (largely in drunkenness and larceny), but that this is more the result of the cultural transmission of attitudes rather than the direct learning of behavior patterns. Moreover, and more interesting from the standpoint of making criminological theory more responsive to changing crime rates, McCord concludes that, overall, the sons in her sample were no more criminal than their fathers, thereby agreeing with the outline of Pepinsky's idea that recording and discovery of crime may be independent of actual behavior.

Although McCord's data are not sufficiently sensitive to give a complete picture (she is very careful not to generalize beyond her data), and although she prefers a sociological, Chicago school explanation for the findings she does detect, the results of this study may also relate to the general point made by Hippchen: since the sample was purposefully selected to be fathers and sons, the findings cannot rule out the importance of biological interaction with social learning.

THEORY APPLICATIONS

James Garofalo's paper on the importance of time in criminological theories raises a number of questions and issues. Many criminological theories stress explicitly the "active" components of social life in descriptions of "becoming" criminal. Unfortunately, many pieces of research fail to take this aspect into account in their "tests" of theories. Garofalo argues that more attention must be devoted to this important dimension in theory testing, and that certain basic problems of longitudinal research will have to be solved before this can be done. Garofalo is well aware of the problems of the proposed research emphasis he suggests here; but he is also aware that they need correcting. The section on recall data is particularly pertinent since many criminologists are relying heavily on self-report and victimization survey results which, in turn, rely on the memory of the respondents. Whether the promise of these data collection techniques will be realized depends on coming to grips with this problem.

The remaining papers in the last section of this volume also deal with promises: the policy promise of the deterrence doctrine, and the theoretical promise of the "payoff" to criminological theory in studying white-collar crime. The last decade has witnessed a resurgence in deterrence research, partly because this area offers some potential for public policy with crime. Unfortunately, the deterrence doctrine remains an a theoretical hypothesis (and a vague one at that) rather than an explicit statement about the relationship between legal sanctions and crime. Minor attempts to remedy this situation by exploring the correspondence between the deterrence doctrine and control theory. Minor finds that the deterrence doctrine is compatible with certain elements of control theory, and that, for some crimes at least, the two perspectives together can inhibit illegality. Perhaps more significant is the suggestion that the deterrence doctrine is a part of existing theories, though not often recognized as such. Minor's paper, then, represents an advance in further specifying the deterrence doctrine, and the conditions under which both legal and extralegal factors can inhibit deviance.

Like the promise of self-reported and victimization data on crime, the promise of studying white-collar crime has been oft stated with little actual delivery. Clark and Hollinger attempt to set forth some conditions which would make this promise a reality. They do so by (1) calling for the conceptualization of this type of crime in terms of occupational and organizational contexts, and (2) by discussing some of the more nagging methodological and ethical problems associated with the kind of research their conceptualization demands. Those who may be surprised at the lack of systematic work on this topic should read particularly those sections which deal with the different unit of observation and analysis this topic requires, and the ill-prepared manner in which most criminologists have approached the problems described by Clark and Hollinger. Still, these atuhors are "cautiously" optimistic about overcoming these problems and the eventual development of this area.

To an extent, this same tone is perhaps characteristic of all of the papers in this volume—an optimism tempered by the kind and amount of work yet to be done, yet there nonetheless. The discipline of criminology, as noted at the outset, is relatively primitive by some standards, and to claim otherwise would be dishonest. This observation is neither praiseworthy nor condemnatory; merely frank. The vitality of criminology lies in the diversity of viewpoints and research of its practitioners, the ingenuity of better minds, and the challenge of those problems which are the subject of this volume.

NOTES

1. In a review essay, Edward Tiryakian (1977) has called Durkheim "buffs" a "growing legion," and has referred to the publication of three volumes of Durkheim's *Textes* as being "required reading for some time to come."

2. I have been able to find only one source (Quinney and Waldman, 1977:50) in a cursory reading of recent criminology texts which acknowledges the fact that perhaps Lombroso had been given too much credit in this regard.

REFERENCES

ECKLAND, B.K. (1967). "Genetics and sociology: A reconsideration." American Sociological Review, 32:173-194.

MEIER, R.F. (1976). "The new criminology: Continuity in criminological theory." Journal of Criminal Law and Criminology, 67:461-469.

MEIER, R.F., and GEIS, G. (1977). "Is criminology a policy science? Journal of Sociology and Social Welfare (in press).

QUINNEY, R., and WALDMAN, J. (1976). The problem of crime: A critical introduction to criminology (2nd ed.). New York: Harper and Row.

SHAW, S.A., and ROTH, L.H. (1974). "Biological and psychophysiological factors in criminality." P. 101-173 in D. Glaser (ed.), Handbook of criminology. Chicago: Rand McNally.

TIRYAKIAN, E.A. (1977). "On discovering Durkheim." Contemporary Sociology, 6:17-19.

Van Den BERGHE, P. (1975). Man in society. New York: Elsevier.

WILSON, E.O. (1975). Sociobiology: The new synthesis. Cambridge: Harvard University Press.

Raymond J. Michalowski
*University of North Carolina
at Charlotte*

1

PERSPECTIVE AND PARADIGM
Structuring
Criminological Thought

It is beginning to appear as if the 1970s will be characterized as
a period of questioning and change for criminology. The emergence of the "new criminology" has generated increased attention to the structure of criminological thought itself as various
criminologists attempt to advance the newer radical paradigm,
defend or update the traditional one, or simply analyze the
contemporary paradigm conflict. Some have based their analysis
upon dichotomous distinctions such as right-left (Miller, 1973),
positivist-power/conflict (Reasons, 1975) or liberal positivist-
socialist (Platt, 1973). The majority, however, have focused
upon a tripartite version of criminological thought variously
comprised of functionalist, symbolic interactionist, and conflict
paradigms (Simecca and Lee, 1974), personality, cultural, and
structural orientations (Wolfgang, 1973), positivist, reformist,
and human rights definitions (Schwendinger and Schwendinger,
1970), value-free science, objective law, and state morality
perspectives (Grabiner, 1973), positivist, social reaction and
conflict theories (Taylor et al., 1973) or conservative, liberal-
cynical and radical criminologies (Gibbons and Garabedian,
1972). Quinney (1973), it should be noted, presents his analysis
of criminological thought based on a *fourfold* classification
involving positivist, interactionist, phenomenological, and critical orientations.

Whether based upon dichotomous, trichotomous, or fourfold distinctions in criminological thought, these analyses share two common characteristics. The various orientations discussed are given as nearly mutually exclusive, and the primary emphasis is upon "paradigms" as they define the content of criminological research, rather than as they are defined by larger social arrangements and ideological forces. The one exception to this is Simecca and Lee (1974) who attempt to link paradigmatic shifts in criminology with changes in the larger social world.

The analysis also examines the structure of criminological thought, and in that sense is built upon the work of others who have examined this question. It differs somewhat, however, in that it focuses first of all on the distinction between *social perspectives* and *scientific paradigms*, and secondly upon the content of, and interaction between, the paradigms derived from each general perspective. It is hoped that this analysis will serve to further explicate the relationship between social forces, social thought and the "scientific" study of crime and deviance.

CRIME, PERSPECTIVE AND PARADIGM

"The true system, the real system, is our present construction of systematic thought itself, rationality itself, and if a factory is torn down but the rationality which produced it is left standing, then that rationality will simply produce another factory. If a revolution destroys a systematic government, but the systematic patterns of thought that produced that government are left intact, then those patterns will repeat themselves in the succeeding government. There's so much talk about the system. And so little understanding."

Robert M. Pirsig
Zen and the Art of Motorcycle Maintenance

Our understanding of reality is not simply a loose collection of unrelated meanings assigned to the events and objects in our environment. It is a more or less systematically organized hierarchy of meanings through which we understand and interpret the world. Although not perfectly organized, the individual components of this hierarchy tend to be relatively consistent with one another. Overall, this logically interrelated hierarchy functions somewhat like a formula for interpreting reality. New experiences are evaluated in terms of this formula and assigned a meaning which is fairly consistent with it. Furthermore, this formula can be said to have certain organizing principles which guide the evaluation of specific experiences.

The manner in which individuals respond to any particular occurrence will be fairly consistent with the key organizing principles of their overall understanding of how the world operates. For the agnostic physician the inexplainable cure of a seemingly fatal disease may represent a "spontaneous remission," while for the devoutly religious patient it may represent a "miracle." in each of these cases the inexplainable cure is defined in a manner consistent with certain organizing principles. One key organizing principle of the agnostic physician's understanding of the world is a relatively mechanical view of the human body, and another is the scientific belief that physical effects have physical causes, even if we cannot identify them. For the religious patient, a key organizing principle is the existence of a knowing and concerned god who is directly involved in the daily affairs of individuals. In each case these organizing principles guide the individuals in their efforts to assign meaning to an event in their lives.

This hierarchy of meanings and the organizing principles from which they are generated is what we mean by the term *perspective*. A perspective is more than just its organizing principles, however. It can be likened to a multifaceted prism with its organizing principles at the center surrounded by the various interpretations of "reality" generated by these principles—the facets. The greater the number of events interpreted according to these organizing principles, the greater the number of facets— i.e., specific meanings—contained within the perspective. Perspectives may vary in scope depending upon the range of events to which they are applicable. However, whether they are broad or relatively narrow in scope, it is through the prism of perspectives that we view reality, and like prisms they color our understanding of the world around us.

While perspectives influence the way we understand the world, we are often not fully conscious of their existence or their effects. Everyday reality is a taken-for-granted reality.[1] Only in specialized contexts do we normally question whether what we understand as reality is really so. For the most part, we assume that it is and respond accordingly.

One of the specialized contexts in which we do question whether everyday reality is as it seems is that of "scientific" inquiry. Here we question the taken-for-granted everyday world. We poke it; we prod it; we turn it over; we try to see its backside and its underside. All of this is done to determine if it is what it seems to be; if it actually operates as the taken-for-granted reality suggests that it will. But even in this context we are not free of the prismatic influence of perspective.

Our scientific understanding, like our understanding of the everyday world, is also the product of certain organizing principles. At the level of scientific inquiry, general perspectives on how that particular part of the world being studied functions leads to the development of relatively consistent bodies of knowledge which reflect the accumulation of past applications of that perspective to a particular phenomenon. As this "scientifically" produced body of knowledge about a particular phenomenon begins to grow and coalesce into a relatively consistent set of understandings, it becomes a *paradigm*—a body of "universally recognized scientific achievements that for a time provide model problems and solutions to a community of practitioners" (Kuhn, 1970:viii).

Paradigms differ from perspectives in that they tend to be narrower in scope, resulting primarily from the study of a particular category of phenomenon, e.g., physical events, chemical reactions, social relations, etc. Also, because they represent the application of organizing principles to the process of "scientific" inquiry they tend to be more extensive and more technical with respect to a particular phenomenon than general perspectives regarding that same phenomenon. They are similar, however, in that each maintains at its core a set of organizing principles which will influence the conclusions drawn and the "discoveries" made, because, as Kuhn observes, they provide the "problems" to be studied as well as the type of solutions found.

While paradigms in their pure form may represent "universally recognized" models for examining problems, in reality they are generally somewhat less than universal. Even within the limited scientific community of practitioners concerned with a particular phenomenon there often exist different paradigms with varying numbers of adherents. At the present time this is particularly true of the study of crime.

The body of what is widely accepted and understood by those studying crime has changed frequently since the earliest scholarly inquiries into its nature. At times divergent paradigms have existed side-by-side with the proponents of each attempting to establish the "rightness" of their particular formula for discerning the nature of crime. At other times a single view has come to predominate and direct our thinking about crime.

At the everyday level our understanding of crime is most strongly influenced by those perspectives which explain the general nature of social organization, and particularly the relationship of law to that organization. At the level of scientific inquiry, our understanding of crime is influenced by paradigms which specify the appropriate focus and method for criminological study. Any critical understanding of criminological theory must first begin with an examination of the perspectives and paradigms, and their organizing principles which have produced this "theory."

PERSPECTIVES ON LAW AND SOCIAL ORGANIZATION

The earliest scholarly investigations into the nature of crime were almost solely concerned with the relationship between law and social organization. During the "classical" period of criminology extending from the late 18th to the late 19th century, writers such as Bentham (1843) and Beccaria (1809) sought to identify the social rules which explained the existence of law and its impact upon the individual members of society. With the advent of the "scientific" study of human behavior, the relationship between law and society became much less of a focal concern for criminologists. The "positive" school of criminology which emerged during the latter part of the 19th century was characterized by a primary emphasis upon understanding the criminal, rather than understanding the nature, source, and effect of law. (Vold, 1968:27-40). While there have been exceptions all along, from the emergence of the "positive" school of criminology until the middle of the 20th century, the "criminal" has been the main focus for the scientific study of crime. Since the 1960s, however, there has reemerged an emphasis on law and society. While the primary emphasis is still upon understanding the criminal, in recent years many criminologists have once again begun to recognize the critical role of law in determining the nature of crime. Furthermore, many have begun to recognize that one's view of the relationship between law and social organization will have an important impact upon subsequent criminological investigations.

The major perspectives which have been utilized to explain the relationship between law and society can be characterized as the *consensus, pluralist,* and *conflict* models of social organization. Each reflects somewhat different organizing principles and different values about the nature of man and society, and each suggests different directions for the study of crime. Considered in terms of political philosophies these three perspectives— consensus, pluralist and conflict—can be viewed along a continuum moving from Right to Left, or from Conservative to Radical:

Consensus	Pluralist	Conflict
(Conservative)	(Liberal)	(Radical)

While we can only discuss these perspectives as separate categories of thought, in practice criminological writings are often *more or less* representative of a particular perspective, combining parts of each in their explanation of some aspect of the crime problem. However, they will generally only incorporate parts of adjacent perspectives. While they may reflect parts of a concensus and a pluralist perspective, or parts of a pluralist and a conflict perspective, it is less likely for specific investigations to reflect a combination of both a concensus and a conflict perspective.

Consensus, Pluralist, and Conflict Models

1. *A Concensus Model.* The consensus model of law and social organization is a derivative of the more general consensus model of society which is a basic theme in the American system of values. The organizing principles or assumptions of the *general* consensus model are: (1) society is a relatively persistent stable structure; (2) society is well integrated; and (3) a functioning social structure is based on a consensus of values (Dahrendorf, 1958:174). When applied specifically to the question of law and social organization, the organizing principles of a consensus model are:

(1) *Law reflects the collective will of the people.* All members of a society agree upon the basic definitions of right and wrong, and the law is merely the written statement of this collective agreement.

(2) *The law serves all people equally.* Because it reflects the collective will of all the people, the law neither serves nor represses the interests of any particular group of individuals.

(3) *Those who violate the law represent a unique subgroup.* Because the majority agree upon the definitions of right and wrong, the small group who violate the law must share some common element which distinguishes them from the law abiding majority.

A consensus model assumes that law reflects general agreement concerning at least the basic elements of social life. This agreement, forged out of the need to establish a persistent, stable, and well-integrated social system, evolves first as mutually shared and agreed upon ways of conducting social interaction—"customs"—which are later formulated into written laws. Although seldom *articulated* in the contemporary study of law, crime, and justice, the consensus perspective has had a major impact on the development of the positivist paradigm, as will be discussed below. Its most common, and most important, application is as a justification for laws and law enforcement.

The entire legal basis of our democratic society as well as our system of crime control is based on the assumption that laws and their enforcement represent what "the people" want. It is a reflection of their collective will.

2. *A Pluralist Model.* A pluralist model reflects a somewhat more complicated view of society. While the consensus model assumes the existence of general agreement upon basic values and interests, a pluralist model recognizes the existence of a multiplicity of social groups which have at times different and competing interests and values. Law exists, within a pluralist model, not because individuals generally agree upon a definition of right and wrong, but precisely because they do not agree. Recognizing the need for some mechanism for conflict resolution, individuals agree upon a legal structure within which conflicts can be resolved without seriously jeopardizing the overall welfare of society. As Chambliss and Siedman (1971:51) note:

> It is a popular viewpoint of present-day political theory in the United States, that while society is no doubt made up of interest groups with divergent goals and values, it is in everybody's interest to maintain a political framework which permits these conflicts to be resolved through peaceful bargaining, always reserving the right of the minority group through peaceful persuasion and dissent.

According to this perspective, conflict exists around substantive disagreements while there exists general consensus about the nature and operation of law and justice. Thus, the basic organizing principles of a pluralist perspective are:

(1) *Society is composed of diverse social groups.* This diversity results from the presence of regional, economic, religious, sex, age, race and ethnic variations in the population.

(2) *There exists among these groups differing, and sometimes conflicting, definitions of right and wrong.* The various groups have different values, goals, and interests, and at times these may come into conflict with one another.

(3) *There is collective agreement on the mechanisms for dispute settlement.* All groups agree upon the establishment of a legal system

within which these conflicts can be peacefully settled.

(4) *The legal system is value-neutral.* The legal mechanisms for dispute settlement are above the disputes themselves. The legal system exists simply as a value-free framework or arena in which the disputes can be *fairly* and peacefully settled.

(5) *The legal system is concerned with the best interests of the society.* While it stands above the specific value-laden disputes between individual social groups, the legal system's overriding concern is with the general well being of the society as a whole. It contributes to this well being by providing a peaceful forum for conflict settlement.

This perspective has had a major impact upon American political thought in the 20th century and is the basis for much of our concern with individual rights and the role of discretion in the administration of justice. It has also substantially contributed to the development of the interactionist paradigm for the study of crime.

3. *A Conflict Model.* A conflict model of law and justice, like the consensus model, is derived from a larger overall perspective on the nature of society. This larger conflict perspective assumes that: (1) at every point society is subject to change, (2) it displays at every point dissensus and conflict, (3) every element contributes to change, and (4) it is based on the coercion of some of its members by others (Dahrendorf, 1958:174). As a model for the study of law and society, the conflict perspective emphasizes the coercive and repressive nature of the legal system. The legal system is not viewed as an impartial tool for dispute settlement, but rather as a mechanism for those with the greatest amount of political power to advance their own interests. At any given time, law reflects neither a general consensus about values, nor a mutually agreed upon mechanism for the settlement of dispute. It represents the interests of those with the power to make and enforce the law, without particular regard for the interests of those without such power or for the best interest of society as a whole. One of the major interests of those with the power to make and enforce the law is the maintenance of this power. As a result, the law

not only serves to advance specific interests of those in power, but also serves to advance their general interest in retaining power. Power is maintained and the interests of those with this power are advanced by defining as criminal those behaviors which conflict with these interests.

The organizing assumptions of a conflict perspective are:

(1) *Society is composed of diverse social groups.*

(2) *There exist differing definitions of right and wrong.* Social groups have diverse values, goals, and interests, and at times these conflict with one another.

(3) *The conflict between social groups is one of political power.* At all times there is an imbalance of political power, with those who have it struggling to maintain it, and those who do not have it struggling to obtain it.

(4) *Law is designed to advance the interests of those with the power to make it.* The law is not a value-neutral forum for dispute settlement. It is a mechanism for those with the power to make the law to advance their own interests, without particular concern for the overall good of the society.

(3) *A key interest of those with the power to make and enforce the law, is maintaining their power.* Much of law is concerned with keeping those with interests different from those in power from gaining political power.

Both the conflict perspective and the pluralist perspective agree that society is comprised of diversity and this diversity leads to conflict between social groups. However, these two perspectives disagree over how such conflicts are resolved. According to the pluralist perspective they are solved by the development of a mutually agreed upon, value-neutral legal system. According to the conflict perspective they are never really resolved, except for the fact that one group may acquire sufficient power to force its will upon others. It is difficult to consider a conflict model of criminal law without reference to the factors which determine political power. The key factor in this determination is the class structure of society. As a result, actual applications of a conflict perspective are oriented toward an analysis of the socioeconomic relationships which determine who has access to the law. This orientation is the essential foundation of the socialist paradigm in contemporary criminology.

PARADIGMS FOR STUDYING CRIME

"Scientific" studies of crime (as opposed to our everyday understanding of crime) generally reflect the organizing principles of one of three paradigms. These paradigms—the *positivist, interactionist,* and *socialist*—consist of specific rules for the conduct of scientific inquiry and at the same time reflect the influence of broader perspectives on the nature of human social organization. While to some extent paradigms are based upon the "knowledge" accumulated by attempts to understand a problem through a particular perspective, once this body of "knowledge" becomes sufficiently developed to serve as a basis for more in-depth investigation, the emerging paradigm develops characteristics and organizing principles of its own. Thus when compared to the perspective(s) which may have influenced their development, paradigms represent distinct ways of interpreting events.

Because they suggest the appropriate problems for study, as well as the methods with which to conduct this study, paradigms influence the nature of scientific "discoveries." This is particularly true in the study of social phenomenon such as crime. Our understanding of the social world is largely dependent upon the way we interpret the events we experience. It is unlikely that our "scientific" research can uncover phenomenon not already included in our understanding of society. In this sense, the paradigm utilized for study will constrict the possible range of findings for any piece of social science research. At the same time, paradigms are useful for organizing the elements of the social world in such a way as to permit the development of specific questions about that world. Like a telescopic lens, they make obscure phenomenon easier to see; but also like a lens, they tend to distort our vision. The things we focus on become larger and other things disappear from the picture altogether.

Of the three major paradigms for studying crime, the positivist most emphasizes the orderliness of social life. The findings it has produced are also the most accepted outside the community of scientific researchers. This acceptance is due, in part, to the fact that the positivist paradigm is derived from the consensus perspective, and it is this perspective which most closely reflects the conventional, everyday understanding of law, crime, and social organization. The interactionist paradigm emphasizes the social-psychological complexity of human life, and since its emergence within criminology in the early 1960s has had a significant impact upon the way many social scientists view crime. Its impact upon the way social agencies and the general public view crime has been less than positivist-oriented research. However, it has been gaining strength in the public domain over the last several years as the scientific "discoveries" of the last decade become the commonplace understandings of the present one. The socialist paradigm emphasizes the economic and political nature of social life. It is the newest and least developed of the three paradigms for studying crime. Unlike the other two, its solutions to the crime problem demand a radical restructuring of society, and for this reason it is at the present time the least favored paradigm both among criminologists and the general public.

Positivist, Interactionist and Socialist Paradigms.

1. *The Positivist Paradigm.* From an historical perspective, positivism refers to the rise of science and the decline of religion as basis for understanding the world. It represents the substitution of "natural" explanations of why events occur for "supernatural" ones (Albrow, 1974:186). Positivism is characterized by a belief in a scientific method which views all occurrences as the result of certain cause-effect relationships. These cause-effect relationships constitute natural laws which govern behavior in both the physical and the social world. The inability to understand certain phenomena from a positivist viewpoint occurs only because we have failed to uncover the laws which govern them.

As a paradigm for the study of crime, positivism emphasizes the determinate nature of human individuals. Human behavior is the result of cause-effect relationships between individuals and some aspect(s) of their environment, and these relationships have a law-like quality. Furthermore, it assumed that these natural laws of human behavior operate for all individuals. That is, individuals who share similar experiences will tend to behave in similar manners. This assumption has particular relevance for the development of crime control strategies. If human behavior is the result of certain cause-effect laws, and these laws affect all individuals similarly, then uncovering these laws will enable a society to both effectively predict under what conditions crime is likely to occur, and to control these conditions. As a result, the positivist paradigm has been extensively employed by those concerned with predicting and controlling criminal behavior.

Positivism also emphasizes the unity of the scientific method and the value-neutrality of science. The scientific method through which we have uncovered "laws" in the physical universe is assumed to be equally applicable to the study of human behavior. This scientific method, in turn, centers around the study of "factual" or "empirical" data. Only those things which we can see, feel, or touch—or which can be measured by something which we can see, feel, or touch—are assumed to be sufficiently "real" to warrant a place in the process of scientific inquiry. Subjective impressions, personal values, and personal feelings do not enter into true "scientific" inquiry—or so it is assumed within the positivist paradigm. Positivism accepts the proposition that it is possible to separate the social scientist and his own personal values from the social world being studied. Positivism is based upon the assumption that there is an absolute separation between the scientist and the thing being studied, i.e., phenomenon can be studied as *real things* outside of our subjective interpretation of them. This assumption of scientific *objectivity*, however, can only be maintained if we take the position that what is being studied is a type of *object* with a permanent and stable character which is not altered by what we think about it. If we are studying a stable object, our conclusions about it may be right or wrong, but the object remains the same regardless. On the other hand, if the very character of what we are studying depends upon what we think about it, it is not possible to uncover the "laws" which govern its behavior.

At the present time there is some debate as to whether the phenomena of crime can be studied as a stable *object*, or whether it is essentially a shifting social idea whose character depends upon what we think about it. That is, while iron, for example, remains iron whether or not we understand its properties, "crime" has no basic properties other than our subjective interpretations of right and wrong. Because crime is a social rather than a physical reality, some argue that it is not possible to study crime as an object, and therefore the positivist claim to objectivity is illusory.

Since it views crime as an object and seeks to uncover the *laws* governing criminal behavior, positivism can most easily focus upon the criminal as the phenomenon to be studied. It is here that the relationship between the positivist paradigm and a consensus model of law and social organization becomes evident. Within the consensus perspective criminals represent a unique subgroup because they fail to live according to the standard definitions of right and wrong agreed upon and followed by the majority of society's members. The positivist paradigm's acceptance of the criminal as the *thing* to be studied similarly suggests that the unique aspect of crime—the thing to be explained—is, "why do a few differ from all the rest?" For the most part positivist criminology accepts the law as a given and focuses simply upon those who violate it; why the law exists and whom it serves are seldom questions for a positivist study of crime. Its link to the consensus perspective has already answered these questions: The law exists because "the people" want it to exists, and it serves all of "the people."

It is because of its link to the consensus perspective that positivism tends to view crime and deviance as *unique properties of individual* and to suggest that the primary focus for study and the primary location for solutions to the crime problem must be the criminal. Positivism alone does not necessarily demand that criminals be the focus of study. It is positivist criminology's link with a consensus perspective that has dictated that the bulk of modern criminological study reflects attempts to understand the uniqueness of the criminal.

As a set of organizing principles for the study of crime and deviance the positivist paradigm can be described as follows:

(1) *Human behavior results from law-like cause and effect relationships.* Human behavior is determined by these relationships and is therefore relatively predictable once these relationships are understood.

(2) *The cause-effect relationships which govern human behavior can be discovered through the same scientific method used to understand the natural, physical environment.* This scientific method emphasizes criminality as a relatively stable object, focuses upon "objective" and quantifiable data and is assumed to be value-free.

(3) *Criminals represent a unique set of cause-effect relationships.* The behavior of criminals is objectively different from the behavior of noncriminals and therefore must represent a different set of cause-effect relationships.

(4) *Once the special cause-effect relationships governing criminal behavior are known, criminal behavior can be predicted and controlled and criminals themselves can be changed.* The study of crime then can be broken down into small units and pragmatic solutions devised for particular segments of the problem.

2. The Interactionist Paradigm. The interactionist paradigm emphasis is that deviance is not a unique quality of individuals; but rather that it is a quality which resides in an observer's response to the behavior of some individuals. In other words, criminality is in the eye of the beholder; certain acts are "criminal" because we define them as such and then respond accordingly. If an act is criminal because of the quality of the response to it, (not because of the quality of the "criminal") we cannot understand crime by simply seeking to identify the cause-effect relationships which determine criminal behavior in the positivist sense. We must look at the interaction process between doer and observer which eventually results in the "label" of criminal being affixed to individuals who engage in certain behaviors.

The interactionist paradigm rejects the positivist notion that criminals are necessarily unique human types governed by unique cause-effect relationships. The only thing unique about criminals may be the manner in which they are treated. In this sense, the interactionist paradigm emphasizes the relativity of criminal behavior. There are no absolute rights or wrongs, nor is there necessarily a relatively stable consensus of values. There is only the interactive process through which labels are affixed to certain behaviors.

This concern with the interactive process leading to "labeling" certain individuals as criminal reflects a view of the "self" as a social construct. Our behaviors and our understanding of ourselves are seen as the result of the ways in which other individuals react to us. When applied to the study of criminal behavior, this suggests that individuals may engage in criminal acts in part because they have been treated by other individuals as if they were "criminals."

A primary focus of the interactionist research has been upon the role of "labeling" in producing deviance. If individuals acquire their self definitions from the way in which others treat them, the very things we do to control criminals—catching, ajudicating, punishing, and rehabilitating—the interactionist argue, may help insure their future criminality. The individual rule-breaker may not be particularly committed to a deviant identity, however, once he has been singled out as "different," he may begin to see himself in those same terms (Lemert, 1951).

The interactionist paradigm reflects the pluralistic assumption that society is comprised of multiple and diverse world views. At a practical level many interactionists also reflect the pluralist concern for a value-free legal system. Concern with discretionary justice which may lead to the more frequent labeling of individuals from certain groups as criminals reflects the pluralist emphasis upon value-neutrality in the administration of justice. This is particularly true for analyses which treat such discretion as a deviation from the ideal of justice rather than as an integral part of the system.[2] The interactionist criminology has also been influenced to a more limited degree by the conflict perspective insofar as the concern with the effects of labeling is supported by the conflict perspective's implication that certain social groups possess greater power to affix labels to others.

The organizing principles of the interactionist perspective can be described as follows:

(1) *Criminality is a quality which resides not in the behavior, but in the response to it.* Behavior is criminal only because actual or potential observers respond to it as such.

(2) *Behaviors responded to as criminal are given the label of criminal.* By responding to a behavior as criminal we designate it as being different from other categories of behavior.

(3) *The individual whose behavior is labeled as criminal is also labeled criminal.* The quality of criminal attached to a particular behavior is generalized to include the individuals who engaged in it. Thus, not only is the behavior viewed as different, the individual is also viewed as different from other categories of individuals.

(4) *Individuals are labeled as criminal through a process of interaction.* Labels can only be affixed through an interactive process involving both the observer and the doer. As a result similar behaviors can result in different labels depending upon the nature of the interaction and the character of the participants.

(5) *There is a tendency for individuals labeled as criminal to identify with that label.* This identification will lead to persistence in behavior which may not have reoccurred if it were never labeled.

3. *A Socialist Paradigm.* Recent years have seen the emergence of a new paradigm within criminology which is variously referred to as critical criminology, radical criminology, Marxist criminology, and socialist criminology. As developed among American criminologists it reflects certain aspects of the conflict perspective. However, while the conflict perspective views conflict as *endemic* to social organization and does not identify a single cause for this conflict, the socialist paradigm pinpoints the capitalist economic system as the source of social conflict, and suggests that conflict is not a necessary condition of human social life. Within this paradigm, as within the conflict perspective, behaviors are defined and treated as crime because they

threaten the interests of the power-dominant group. For the socialist paradigm, however, this dominant group is specifically the capitalist ruling class—those who own and control the means of production. Similarly the socialist paradigm accepts the conflict perspective's assumption that a primary use of the legal system by those in power is maintenance of their power advantage. Indeed, the political state is created, according to the socialist paradigm, to serve the interests of the capitalist ruling class and to preserve their ruling position.

The socialist paradigm differs significantly from the conflict perspective also in its acceptance of an absolute standard of justice. Crime is not simply a matter of who has the power to define criminal behavior. Regardless of what behaviors are defined as criminal, true crimes are those activities which violate the egalitarian human rights to decent food and shelter, to human dignity, and to self-determination (Schwendinger and Schwendinger, 1970). Thus, in addition to examining how those behaviors normally defined as crime come to be so defined within a capitalist political economy, the socialist paradigm also examines systems of human exploitation not normally defined as crime. Imperialism, racism, sexism, and similarly structured exploitations become the focus for criminological investigation, as well as the relationship of more standard crime to the capitalist society (Platt, 1974:6).

For the most part the socialist paradigm rejects the individual offender as the appropriate focus for criminological research in favor of a primary focus on the overall structure of the society. In this sense the socialist paradigm differs markedly from both the positivist and the interactionist, which study primarily the offender or the offender and his labeler, respectively. The socialist paradigm also asserts the value-based nature of science. It rejects positivist (and in some cases the interactionist) claims of value-neutrality, and argues instead that such claims simply mask a commitment to the underlying assumptions of the status quo value system.

The basic organizing principles of the socialist paradigm are:

(1) *The capitalist political state exists to preserve the interests of the dominant economic class—those who own and control the means of*

production. While the capitalist ruling class may not directly control the daily operations of the political state, they have a disproportionate control over the decisions of that state.

(2) *The primary interest of the capitalist ruling class is the maintenance of an economic and social order which preserves their power and privilege*. The political state is directed by the capitalist ruling class to treat, both practically and ideologically, behaviors which threaten the existing economic and political order as the most serious harms in society.

(3) *The primary purpose of criminal law is to maintain an economic and social order advantageous to the ruling elites by criminalizing behaviors which threaten this order*. As a result the primary focus of criminal law is on behaviors which threaten either the current distribution of property or the state's monopoly on the right to use force.

(4) *Behaviors which threaten the domestic order are controlled through a criminal justice system operated by "law-workers" who serve the interests of the capitalist ruling class*. While these law-workers are not themselves part of the ruling class, they have accepted the ideology of the ruling class.

(5) *The Contradictions of the capitalist state require that the disadvantaged classes, especially the propertyless underclass, be controlled through the force represented by the legal system*. For this reason the criminal justice system is used most frequently and most forcefully against the poor and disenfranchised who violate the law.

(6) *The problems of crime in a capitalist society can only be solved through a collapse of the capitalist state and the emergence of a new society based on socialist principles.*

Points of Convergence

Up to this point the various thought systems influencing contemporary criminology have been treated as relatively discrete orientations. It should be noted, however, that in practice, criminological research is only more or less guided by the organizing principles of a specific paradigm and its related perspective(s). Criminologists have often borrowed from and blended the organizing principles of adjacent perspectives and paradigm in attempting to examine some particular aspect of the crime problem. Some examples of this type of synthesis are Sutherland's differential association theory and the "labeling" approach to deviant behavior.

Differential association theory did not *directly* question the existence of a dominant consensus of values, but at the same time it partially accepted the more pluralist orientation by recognizing the existence of alternative value systems, the acceptance of which could evolve through *normal* learning processes (Sutherland, 1947:4-9). Similarly, while differential association theory accepted—to some degree—the uniqueness of the criminal as suggested by a consensus perspective, and reflected the positivist emphasis upon researching the criminal, these orientations were tempered somewhat by the influence of pluralist and interactionist concepts. The criminal was seen as only quasi-unique; deviant in his or her behavior but average with respect to the learning processes leading to that behavior. Thus, differential association theory represented a somewhat lesser commitment to the organizing principles of a consensus perspective and a positivist paradigm than did earlier research attempting to locate criminality within individual biology.

Another example of this type of thought system blending is the labeling perspective, particularly as it was reflected in a concern with the differential application of labels.[3] Research of this type accepted both the pluralist assumption of existing multiple world views and the interactionist view of the self as social process. At the same time there was also reflected the conflict perspective's concern with the differential power of certain social groups to design and affix labels to those lacking this power. Becker (1963:135-146), for example, concerns himself both with the interactive process leading to accepting the label of "marijuana user" and the creation of marijuana use as a legally stigmatized activity. The labeling orientation, for the most part, has always reflected an uneasy admixture of pluralist and conflict perspectives. The conflict perspective's emphasis upon the role of differential power in criminalization is evident in the labeling perspective. At the same time, however, concerns with the discretionary and discriminatory aspects of labeling were also influenced by the pluralist notion that the legal

system *ought* to function as a value-free forum for the settlement of social disputes. As a result, labeling theory verged on
the border of the conflict perspective but never was able to
generate a "structural analysis involving a radical critique of
power and inequality." (Taylor et al., 1973:157).

Another point of convergence which argues against viewing
the perspectives and paradigms discussed as totally unique
thought systems is the fact that they share, in some cases,
similar assumptions. As mentioned previously both the pluralist
and the conflict perspectives emphasize the existence of social
and cultural diversity, although the perceived implications of
this diversity for subsequent legal arrangements vary. Similarly,
both positivist and socialist paradigms accept the existence of
an objective human reality beyond the elements of its social
construciton, although they suggest radically different methods
of understanding this reality. This does not mean that the
difference in impact of these perspectives and paradigms upon
criminological thought is negligible. Each combines the shared
elements with other more unique aspects to create an epistemo-
logically and methodologically different whole. Yet, analysis of
criminological thought should take into account the conver-
gences between different orientations, as well as their diver-
gences.

CONCLUSION

The structure of criminological thought can be viewed not
simply as a matter of divergent scientific paradigms, but also as
a matter of more general and to some extent, parent perspectives on the nature of social organization and its relationship to
law. At the level of perspective, criminological thought hinges
upon critical philosophical distinctions regarding the nature of
man, and it is this level of thought which determines subsequent
orientations to the study of crime.

When viewing the structure of criminological thought, it is
important to incorporate not just the specific paradigms, but
also the more general perspectives on the nature of social order
which they imply. This paper has sought to outline the three

basic perspectives—the consensus, pluralist, and conflict—and the three scientific paradigms—the positivist, interactionist, and socialist—which are extant in the contemporary study of crime. By viewing these various thought systems as located along parallel continua it should be possible to locate specific criminological theories with respect to both their major paradigmatic orientation and the underlying perspective they imply.

NOTES

1. For a comprehensive discussion of the taken-for-granted nature of everyday reality, see Schutz (1962).

2. The concern with the negative implications of discretionary justice for achieving the type of impartiality in law enforcement suggested by a pluralist model is evident in such works as Skolnick (1966), Newman (1956), Chevigny (1969), Reiss (1971), and Davis (1969).

3. See, for example, Becker (1963), Schwartz and Skolnick (1962), Emerson (1969), and Platt (1969).

REFERENCES

ALBROW, M. (1974). "Dialectical and categorical paradigms of a science of society." Sociological Review, 22:183-201.

BECCARIA, C. (1809). Essays on crimes and punishment. New York: Stephen Gould.

BECKER, H.S. (1963). Outsiders. New York: Free Press.

BENTHAM, J. (1843). Principles of penal law. Edinburgh: Edinburgh University Press.

CHAMBLISS, W.J., and SIEDMAN, R. (1971). Law, order and power. Reading, Mass.: Addison-Wesley.

CHEVIGNY, P. (1969). Police power. New York: Pantheon.

DAHRENDORF, R. (1958). "Toward a theory of social conflict." Journal of Conflict Resolution, 2:170-183.

DAVIS, K.C. (1969). Discretionary justice. Urbana, Ill.: University of Illinois Press.

EMERSON, R.M. (1969). Judging delinquents. Chicago: Aldine.

GIBBONS, D.C., and GARABEDIAN, P. (1972). "Conservative, liberal and radical criminology: Some trends and observations." in C. Reasons (ed.), The criminologist: Crime and the criminal. Pacific palisades, Calif.: Goodyear.

GRABINER, G. (1973). "The limits of three perspectives on crime: Value-free science, objective law and state morality." Issues in Criminology, 8:35-49.

KUHN, T.S. (1970). The structure of scientific revolutions. Chicago: University of Chicago Press.

LEMERT, E.M. (1951). Social pathology. New York: McGraw-Hill.

MILLER, W.B. (1973). "Ideology and criminal justice policy: Some current issues." Journal of Criminal Law and Criminology, 64:141-62.

NEWMAN, D. (1956). "Pleading guilty for consideration: A study of bargain justice." Journal of Criminal Law, Criminology and Police Science, 46:780-790.

PLATT, A. (1969). The child savers. Chicago: University of Chicago Press.

——— (1973). "Prospects for a radical criminology in the United States." Crime and Social Justice, 1:2-9.

QUINNEY, R. (1973). "Crime control in capitalist society: A critical philosophy of legal order." Issues in Criminology, 8:75-99.

——— (1974). Criminal justice in America. Boston: Little, Brown.

REASONS, C. (1975). "Social thought and social structure." Criminology, 13:332-365.

REISS, A.J. (1971). The police and the public. New Haven: Yale University Press.

SCHUTZ, A. (1962). Collected papers, I: The problem of social reality. The Hague: Martin Nijhoff.

SCHWARTZ, R.D., and SKOLNICK, J. (1962). "Two studies of legal stigma." Social Problems, 10:133-142.

SCHWENDINGER, H., and SCHWENDINGER, J. (1970). "Defenders of order or guardians of human rights." Issues in Criminology, 5:123-157.

SIMECCA, J., and LEE, S. (1974). "Paradigm changes in criminology and deviance: A sociology of knowledge approach." Paper presented at the American Society of Criminology meetings, November.

SKOLNICK, J. (1966). Justice without trial. New York: John Wiley.

SUTHERLAND, E.H. (1947). Principles of criminology. Philadelphia: Lippincott.

TAYLOR, I., WALTON, P., and YOUNG, J. (1973). The new criminology: For a social theory of deviance. London: Routledge and Kegan Paul.

VOLD, G.B. (1966). Theoretical criminology. New York: Oxford University Press.

WOLFGANG, M.E. (1973). "Developments in criminology in the United States with some comments on the future." Paper presented at the Fifth National Conference, Institute of Criminology, University of Cambridge, England.

Leonard Savitz
Stanley H. Turner
Toby Dickman
Temple University

2

THE ORIGIN OF SCIENTIFIC CRIMINOLOGY
Franz Joseph Gall as the First Criminologist

For a variety of rather fortuitous reasons, it has become a commonplace for academic criminologists to point (occasionally with pride) to Cesare Lombroso as the founder of the field of "scientific" criminology and to automatically assign to him, and to the Positivist school, the crucial achievement of being the first systematic investigator of crime and the criminal. As has already been discussed (Savitz, 1972), the Lombrosian "triumph," in America at least, came about largely as a consequence of a chance association of the newly burgeoning Italian/anthropological/positivist school, with the simultaneous rise in the late 19th century of biological evolutionary thought, racism, and the science of physical anthropology; the scientific aura accruing to these latter noncriminological movements, somehow, reflected onto, and gave a scientific cast to Lombrosianism, which it has, more or less, retained to the present day.

Pre-Lombrosian investigators of criminals and crime patterns have generally been ignored, or at least not seriously considered by virtually all commentators and soi-disant social science historians. Criminology textbooks and volumes purportedly surveying the historical development of criminological theory and research usually blithely leap from the armchair speculations of the "classical" theorists to the research of Lombroso and his school. The early 19th century French environment research of

A.M. Guerry, Quetelet, and others seem simply never to have existed. Even earlier physiological/biological models of criminal behavior, particularly that developed by Franz Joseph Gall and the Phrenological School, are sometimes acknowledged as having existed but then are treated with contempt and summarily dismissed as "non-scientific." On the other hand, De Quiros (1911), Branham and Kutash (1949) and Mannheim (1960) simply omit any discussion of phrenology; Vold (1958) dismisses it as an "abortive absurdity" and Bonger (1936) treats it, en passant, under "Pre-History of Criminology." Goring, in his monumental *The English Convict* (1913), the final nail in the Lombrosian coffin, describes phrenology simply as a "misnamed science."

Upon examination it becomes clear, however, that this complete devaluation of phrenology as being completely unscientific is never based on the authors' considered evaluation of the published work, research, and data developed by Gallian phrenologists. It would seem appropriate to attempt to ascertain if the scientific roots of criminology do truly lie within the Lombrosian school, or if a reasonable case can be made for the priority and superior claim of F.J. Gall and scientific phrenology as the true precursor of modern scientific criminology.

The life of Cesare Lombroso and the growth of the Positivist school has been extensively documented and is sufficiently known to criminologists so as not to require reiteration. The tortuous and peculiar history of phrenological thought and research, however, does merit some exposition.

Franz Joseph Gall was born in Tiefenbrun, Baden, Germany, in 1758 and he studied medicine in Strasbourg and, after 1781, in Vienna where he received his medical degree in 1785. He had early in life been struck by the fact that persons who excelled in language or had superior memories also seemed to have large, prominent eyes and he thus became convinced of the biological linkage between constitution and significant forms of psychological and social behavior. He spent 20 difficult years engaged in surgical experimentations and medical investigations arduously building up an impressive body of data which directed him to develop his theory of derbral localizations. He utilized over the years, of course, all of the scientific devices and apparatuses available to surgeons and medical researchers, and no one has ever seriously questioned the scientific nature and the fundamental value of his anatomical studies. By common consent, he is conceded to be one of the discoverers of the localizations of brain functions and for this alone his place in the history of anatomy and biology seems assured. Erik Nordenskiold in *The History of Biology* describes Gall as "one of the most brilliant anatomists of his age."

As a result of his anatomic research, Gall proceded to theorize that interior cerebral development was closely related to a finite number of brain functions (all with putative weaknesses and strengths) and that the brain physically altered the shape of the cranium. Gall believed:

(1) The brain was the center of thought (probably his most "dangerous" assertion);

(2) Specific brain areas controlled different behavioral activities;

(3) Brain areas (also called "organs," "faculties") of greater importance were greater in size and area;

(4) The skull precisely and accurately covered the cranial cortex, so that organs of disproportionate importance (and disproportionate growth and size) produce concomitant protruberances on the skull.

Gall was *not* interested in the skull per se; measuring the cranium was merely a means of more simply measuring the cortex and its various organs or functions. The skull itself was easier to "get at" and examine than was the interior brain. Gall (Temkin, 1947) said "The object of my researchers is the brain. The cranium is only a faithful cast of the brain and is consequently only a minor part of the principal object." He found 26 discrete functions; his disciple, Spurzheim, divided the brain into 35 organs, and subsequent commentators derived still other numbers. Of fundamental importance to criminologists was the "Destructiveness" organ (slightly over the ear) which was found to be associated with violent criminal behavior, particularly murder. While the number and names often varied, there seems to have been complete agreement among phrenologists as to the name, location, and importance of the Destructiveness organ.

Via his superlative dissecting skills, and within prevailing Baconian scientific practices and tradition, Gall induced his biological theories, originally known as cranioscopy, cranology, zoonomy, and later named phrenology by Thomas I. Forster. (Jacobs, 1971).

Gall published some tentative early findings in 1791 and continued to lecture in Vienna to the end of the century. Early in the 19th century, however, he and his disciple, student, friend, and coauthor—Johann Gaspar Spurzheim—were charged (at the instigation of the Catholic Church) with endangering morality and religion because of the phrenological assertion that the brain, not the heart, was the seat of reason. Manifestly, this was not an original assertion with Gall; Pythagorous and Galen articulated a similar belief two thousand years before. Gall's assertions, however, were based on personal scientific investigations and not on philosophic speculation. Nevertheless, the phrenologists were thought to be Deists, or even worst, Atheists, and were forbidden from further private lecturing. (This religious animus was to dog phrenology in Europe, England, and, most particularly, in the United States.)

Consequently, Gall and Spurzheim left Vienna and journied for several years throughout Europe. The wanderjahre proved most successful. Two medals were struck of Gall in tribute of his Berlin lectures. First Goethe, then St. Simon, seemingly became mesmerized by Gall and they followed him as he went from city to city. Metternich, after attending several lectures, felt compelled to call Gall "the greatest mind" he had ever known. Gall's considerable anatomical skills and talents were clearly recognized by his contemporaries. An Institute de France committee (including such luminaries as Pinel and Cuvier) unanimously confirmed Gall's extraordinary virtuosity as a brain anatomist; they were, however, unwilling to pass judgment on his phrenological theories, which, they hastily described as being "irrelevant" to their particular (Mathematical-Physical) sector of the Institute (Boring, 1929). Gall continued throughout his life to publish research on the brain and nervous system.

The original research and concomitant doctrines of Gall were circulated throughout Europe and America, largely due to a number of extremely dedicated, frequently quite gifted, disciples. The most important of these was Johan Gaspar Spurzheim (1776-1873), originally a student, he soon became a close friend and collaborated with Gall on the first two volumes of *Anatomie et Physiologie. . .* (Gall, 1810-1819). Spurzheim was a writer of great energy, an extremely dynamic personality, and a lecturer of apparently enormous impact. He lectured with great success at the Royal College of Physicians and the Royal Societies of London and Dublin. (Sad to say, he broke with Gall in 1813, probably because of professional jealousies over the relative contribution that he had made to phrenological theory. Gall went on to publish the last two volumes of *Anatomie et Physiologie. . .* as "completed by himself.") Spurzheim's visit to the United States in 1832 was a triumph and he made many converts to the phrenological cause.

In England, there was Charles Combe (1788-1858) who produced the first work on phrenology printed in England, *Essay on Phrenology*, in 1819. Again, he was extremely active and dedicated, but, in fact, he personally developed little that was new. He and Spurzheim disagreed on nomenclature, with one organ being called "inhabitiveness" by Spurzheim and entitled "concentrativeness" by Combe. Combe was offered a chair in "Mental and Moral Philosophy" at the University of Michigan in 1837, but he declined the offer because of Michigan's climate and physical remoteness. He was instrumental in developing phrenological societies in more than half of all the counties in England and in most of the large cities. Phrenology in Great Britain seems not to have caught the fancy of the general public but it did attract many gentlemen scholars who were, at best, an uncertain basis of support. Combe did not claim that phrenology was an "exact" science, but was, rather an "estimate" science, that is, a science with errors. The major scientific personage who accepted phrenology in England was Sir George MacKenzie, fellow of all of the major professional societies and a world famous minerologist and geologist. MacKenzie pleaded that phrenology merely required a fair hearing for wide acceptance, but he felt it was never received (and indeed, there is much justification for his belief). The medical profession, as a whole in the early years of phrenology at least, were favorably disposed to it, despite the curious fact that the brain as the true seat of the mind was not fully accepted by British medical practitioners until 1850 (De Giustino, 1969).

In the United States, the preeminent popularizer was that remarkable physician and advocate of many causes, Charles Caldwell (1772-1853), who wrote the first American textbook on phrenology, *Elements of Phrenology*, in 1824. In this book, Caldwell produced new data supportive of phrenological claims. Thus, he cites one examination of 29 women, guilty of infanticide, who were phrenologically measured; for 27 of the 29, there were found defectively developed philoprogenitiveness organs. Caldwell, along with almost all other phrenologists, emphasized that phrenology was not a deterministic model of behavior. *Will* could control phrenological dispositions; good environment could develop the highest instincts which could inhibit the biological drive to crime. Isaac Ray (1807-1881; one of Mannheim's Pioneers in Criminology), father of modern medical jurisprudence, was originally a phrenologist and early translated two of Gall's publications. Dr. William Physick, unarguably the leading medical figure of his generation, became the first president of the Central Phrenological Society in 1828. Other notable Americans who became involved in the phrenological movement include John Quincy Adams and John Calhoun (both members of the Phrenological Society of Washington), Nicholas Biddle, Horace Mann, Martin Van Buren, William Ellery Channing, George Bancroft, and Noah Webster. Edward Livingston wrote that he believed that certain levels of incorrigible criminals could be identified by phrenological means.

Phrenology's impact was greater and more profound in the United States than it was in Great Britain. It was a science-philosophy embraced by a significant segment of the general population. Due to Caldwell's cajoling, America was visited by both Spurzheim in 1832 and Combe from 1838 to 1840, and they both performed dazzlingly. Emerson, a rather slow man with a superlative, declared that Spurzheim had "one of the world's greatest minds."

But just at this time, the face of the theory was changing. O.S. and L.N. Flower published *Phrenology Proved* in 1837 and this proved so popular that it went through nine editions in three years; consequently the brothers later produced an almost equally successful, *Practical Phrenology*. Unhappily, these "phrenological Fowlers" were representatives of the new, practical, "applied" phrenology which represented a distinct debasement of the phrenological scheme (Vold, 1958). It has been said that where the "science" of Gall and Spurzheim failed to gain a broad-based, popular audience, the applied phrenology of "quacks" succeeded (Davies, 1955).

Phrenologists in England and America were always careful to assert that there was not immutable, fatalistic, or deterministic elements to phrenology, despite its biological roots. Strength of character, will power, and other factors might and could alter bodily drives. In the early years, phrenologists were actively committed to alterations in the criminal law and improvements in corrections. It proved to aid in the identification of *improveable* criminals. Generally, phrenologists approved of the Pennsylvania (solitary) system of penology because any man experiencing such a punishment would do anything rather than repeat "the intolerable pain of solitude and isolation." Phrenologists argued for the abolition of the death penalty which, they argued, could not deter anyone, and they thought that the transportation of criminals served no useful purpose. (Curiously, Alexander Maconachie was, himself, an advocate of phrenology at various times in his life.)

THE DECLINE OF PHRENOLOGY

In England, phrenology lost its original impact and began to dissolve for several reasons:

(1) There arose serious personal conflicts between eminent phrenologists and persons who were able to "mold public opinion." This took largely the form of journalistic hostility to phrenology

generated, not for any rational or scientific reason, but because of interpersonal animosities. Thus George Combe was personally disliked by Francis Jeffrey, editor of the *Edinburgh Review*, who used his hugely influential journal to mount continuing attacks not only on Combe but on phrenology generally.

(2) Few persuasive scientific investigators or even dynamic popularizers arose after Spurzheim and Combe; rather a number of transient spokesmen of little worth came onto the scene, noted primarily for their calculated greed and eccentricities notable even by British standards.

(3) Inevitably, internal conflict arose within the English phrenological movement reflecting disagreements as to politics, personal ambitions, and clashing personalities. Thus, Combe and Spurzheim took a deep dislike to a fellow phrenologist named Elliotson, because of the latter's eccentric appearance: he sported a beard and wore neither silk stockings nor knee breeches.

(4) The movement failed to produce a continuous body of serious data after the early 1830s; the scientific roots of phrenology inevitably withered and died.

(5) In Great Britain, phrenology was taken up as a leisure time pursuit by a number of dilettantish professional men; when a newer, more fashionable "science" arose, they embraced it and, consequently, abandoned phrenology. Thomas Huxley, rather late in life, was asked why he had not been, earlier, a phrenologist. He replied that he had not done so only because no other prominent man of science had been a phrenologist. In this, as in so many other matters, Huxley was palpably in error. Indeed, as late as 1899, Alfred Russell Wallace is quoted as believing that "in the coming century, phrenology will surely gain general acceptance" (Davies, 1955).

In sum, then, it will be seen that almost never was phrenology proven to be unsound or nonscientific. Its demise was not due to any weight of evidence, but to far more prosaic matters of personal animus, fatigue, and the rise of hucksterism.

In the United States phrenology took a somewhat different path:

(1) There were, as in Great Britain, personality conflicts which almost never had to do with the *worth* of phrenology as a science.

(2) Similarly, research declined sharply, but did not altogether disappear. Up to the Civil War, systematic bodies of research were being gathered as to phrenological "peculiarities" of prison inmates. But, it must be admitted, that the scientific thrust of phrenology had ended by the 1840s.

(3) The general public, who were more heavily committed to phrenology in this country than in Great Britain, came to believe that there was an unmodifiable fatalistic nature to biologically-based phrenology. As indicated before, all serious phrenologists, aware of the seriousness of this accusation, denied it to a man. Gall, himself a lifelong pessimist, contended that phrenological factors were not immutable but that will and spirit were basic and they exercised supreme control over human behavior (Vold, 1958).

(4) Of importance also was the fact that the original, more-or-less scientific advocates of phrenology were replaced in the 1840s by rather glib popularizers, such as the Fowlers, and they, in turn, were quickly replaced by out-and-out charlatans. Science was gone and conjecture was in its place. Jacobs (1971) contends that, while American phrenology was comparatively diffused throughout the population by the 1840s, it had lost its scientific quality, which in American science was still something of a heterogenous affair, and that the already present element of popularization gained preeminence. In the end phrenology was driven to telling people how to be happy, how to select a wife, and how to raise children. It became something akin to a contemporary course in Marriage and the Family, and with about the same level of accuracy, we would judge.

(5) There was, inevitably, serious opposition by various religious groups who somehow perceived phrenology to be irreligious, if not positively sacriligious, and this is considered to have caused significant erosion in public support of phrenology. This hostility had no medical or scientific basis but was, as one might imagine, very emotional in its origins and in its expression. "It was not false because it was unproven; it could not be true because it was immoral" (Davies, 1955).

THE SCIENTIFIC BASIS OF PHRENOLOGY

Surprisingly, this is not a difficult issue to deal with. First of all, there can be little serious questioning of the scientific nature and value of Gall's original anatomic research. He was, as has already been seen, widely acknowledged to have engaged in work of lasting importance based upon the rules of scientific inquiry operating at his time. Davies (1955) contends that phrenology originated as an experimental science with the a priori assumption that mental phenomena had natural causes which could be determined. Gall's theory was simply that "anatomical and physiological characteristics have a direct influence upon mental behavior."

De Guistino (1969) argues that phrenology originally was simple and scientific and early phrenologists could be characterized as being "rationalists par excellence"; it was a "visually definite" field of investigation and it dealt with "precise, measurable" data. Boring (1929) believes that Gall had stumbled on the problem of correlation and that he could have chosen a population and measured precisely the skull formations of the subjects (information set I); independently, estimates should have been made of the degree or presence of significant phrenologically-related patterns of behavior, without the knowledge of actual cranial measurements (information set II). Gall then might have determined the correlation between the two information sets. Having argued thusly, Boring recognized that at the time of Gall's research, personal observation and scientific controls depended more on the rigor of individual investigators' practices and beliefs than on any commonly agreed upon set of scientific conventions and practices.

A fair body of scientific phrenological data was summated by Watson in 1830. Fink (1938) cites a number of reasonably sound phrenology researches produced in America. For example, an investigation of all prisoners entering Eastern State Penitentiary (in Philadelphia) from 1856-1865 found, and reported in the 1856 annual report, that 17.3% of all prisoners had highly developed Destructiveness faculties. (There is some evidence that a phrenological "frame of reference" pervaded these reports until 1904). Further, Fink mentions a project carried out with inmates in a St. Louis Jail, which he judged to be "remarkably accurate". Combe, while visiting the United States in the late 1830s, also spent a considerable portion of his time measuring a large number of inmates in various American prisons.

One could continue the list of acceptable investigations which were undertaken by a number of serious phrenologists over a considerable period of time. Commentators have remarked that the decline of phrenology was in some ways "inexplicable" in that the system was based on "able men using the best scientific methods of their day" (Riegel, 1933). Davies (1955) is forced to conclude, after iterating the truism that the science of one generation is the pseudoscience of the next, that the trouble with phrenology was not its late-blooming charlatanism, but rather the "limitations of early 19th century scientific methods."

A COMPARISON OF LOMBROSO AND GALL.

After this comparatively brief introduction to the history of the phrenological movement, perhaps we should compare the Gallian theory with Lombrosian positivism on a number of significant issues to ascertain more appropriately the comparative scientific merits of each.

1. *Priority of Claim*. Lombroso published the first edition of *L'Uomo Delinquente* in 1876, and, of course, the famous second edition two years later. Gall published his first major work, *Craniologie ou Decouvertes Nouvelles. . .* in 1807. Phrenology obviously then preceeded positivism by about 70 years.

2. *General Scientific Reputation of the Respective Theorists*. Prior to *L'Uomo Delinquente*, Lombroso could accurately be described as a competent, hard-working, physician/surgeon/ scientist who had published several books (one on genius, another on pellegra) and a number of articles describing his measurements of prisoners. A man of ability and no small talents, certainly, but not a man of exceptionally high scientific reputation. F.J. Gall, by critical consensus, was internationally recognized as a researcher and brain anatomist of extraordinary talent, bordering, in some opinions, on genius. His place was assured in the history of biology, anatomy, and, arguably, psychology even before he enunciated his phrenological model.

3. *The Explanatory Variable of Each Theory.* Lombroso's original explanation of criminality was the attribution of a cluster of peculiar anatomical-biological-genetic stigmata producing, in some cases, an evolutionary throwback, or atavism. (One might note that from edition to edition, the Lombrosian theory extended dramatically, adding bits and pieces of psychological and sociological factors until, finally, it became a perfectly eclectic melange of dozens of causative elements.) Gall's basic variable was that the weaker and stronger sections of the brain produced or altered some basic forms of human behavior.

4. *The Entitled Theories.* Lombroso's explanation of crime became known as the Italian, the Antrhopological, and, most significantly, as the Positivist theory. Positivism meant that society was susceptible of analysis in purely objective mechanistic terms so that social values and normative standards are merely epiphenomenological. Gall's theory of Cranioscopy was most commonly called Phrenology, which is simply the science of the mind. The attractiveness of the term "positivism" was not an inconsequential factor in the subsequent "triumph" of Lombrosianism.

5. *The Scientific Bases of the Original Theories.* Lombroso spent a number of years closely examining and measuring hundreds of prisoners in various parts of Italy and based on these observations, plus the historic opening of Vilella's skull (with its acclaimed median occipital fossa), he derived his original stigmatic-atavistic model. Gall spent 20 years measuring in precise detail hundreds of brains and skulls before publishing the results of his activities and subsequently enunciating his phrenological theory.

6. *The Use of Scientific Paraphernalia.* This is not, in our judgment, a trivial point. Gall seemingly used all of the devices and tools normally available to scientists and surgeons of his time. Lombroso utilized an incomparably more dramatic array of newly created apparatuses, mostly the inventions of Paul Louis Broca, the physical anthropologist. The popular view of the scientific nature of Lombrosianism was unquestionably enhanced by the marvelous machinery it used.

7. *The Life Period of the Theories.* It seems clear that the

Lombrosian theory was scientifically legitimate from 1876 (the first edition of *L'Uomo Delinquente)* to 1913 (Goring's *The English Convict)*, or a period of 37 years. There are no such clear landmarks with phrenology but it would seem reasonable that phrenology was intellectually viable from about 1807 to 1845, or for approximately 38 years.

8. *Scientific Research Produced to Subsequently Substantiate the Theories.* Gall's primary disciples, Spurzheim and Combe, both engaged in a considerable amount of research relevant to phrenological concerns, and phrenological data was systematically collected and published until about 1865. A number of criminological Politivists, including Ferri, engaged in quite respectable research. (Garofalo philosophized; he did not measure.)

9. *The Nature of the Opposition to the Theories.* Positivism, within the Lombrosian context, simply ceased to function as a serious explanation of crime with the publication of *The English Convict*, which represented the most careful (and devastating) empirical test of Lombroso's theory. (Earlier attacks had been mounted by numerous French Environmentalists, particularly Manouvrier and Lacassagne.) As indicated earlier phrenology seems to have declined for a number of reasons—interpersonal hostilities, a diminishing phrenological passion, religious antagonisms—but almost never was hard data produced which disproved phrenology. Phrenology died not because it was disproven, it expired from other causes.

10. *Adaptability of the Theories to Modern Scientific Knowledge.* Lombroso's asymmetrical stigmas, atavisms, and even his later epileptoid personalities as causal elements producing criminal behavior receives no support from modern science. On the other hand, if we focus on the most criminologically relevant phrenological organ, "Destructiveness," it is of more than passing interest to note that the precise brain area embraced by that faculty, as this was commonly accepted by phrenologists, was directly above the ear (see Figure 1). Modern brain surgery has, admittedly with moderate success, reduced extremely aggressive, uncontrollably hostile behavior in some individuals by destroying very restricted areas of the amygdala

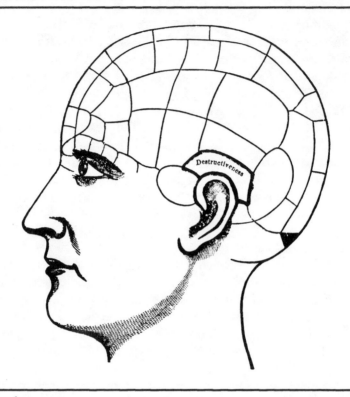

Figure 1:

and the hippocampus (Figure 2) and these are precisely within the "Destructive" organ area. (One might speculate that Gall's anatomical studies of the brain early revealed to him one major area involved in human violent behavior.)

Thus, phrenology preceded positivism by over half of a century. It was enunciated by a scientist of worldwide reputation who, it should be noted, postulated a theory within his own acknowledged area of professional expertise. The techniques and practices used by Gall and his disciples were well within normally accepted scientific rules, beliefs, and procedures operating at the time. The original theory was based on years of painstaking research followed by the continuing data collection of other (admittedly lesser) phrenologists, and it seems never to have been scientifically disproven. Finally, perhaps the most

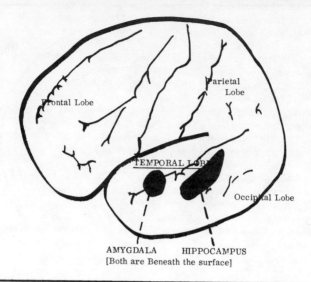

Figure 2: SIDE VIEW OF THE BRAIN

significant criminological aspect of the phrenological theory, with some slight modifications, is not patently absurd within the light of contemporary scientific knowledge.

If the palm for being the originator of scientific criminology were to be given to either Cesare Lombroso or Franz Joseph Gall, and this were to be done on a rational basis, there can be no serious doubt that the award would be granted to Franz Joseph Gall.

REFERENCES

BONGER, W.A. (1936). An introduction to criminology. London: Metheum.

BORING, E.G. (1929). A history of psychology. New York: Century Co.

BRANHAM, V.C., and KUTASH, S.B. (1949). Encyclopedia of criminology. New York: Philosophical Library.

CALDWELL, C. (1824). Elements of phrenology. Lexington, Ky.: Skillman.

——— (1838). Phrenology vindicated and anti-phrenology unmasked. New York: Samuel Coleman.

——— (1833). "Phrenology vindicated, in remarks on article III of the July 1833 number of the *North American Review* headed 'Phrenology.' .. Annals of Phrenology 1:1-102.

COMBE, G. (1822). Essays on phrenology. Philadelphia: Carey and Lea.

——— (1857). On the relation between science and religion. Edinburgh.

——— (1841). Note on the United States of America during a phrenological visit in 1838-1839-1840 (2 volumes). Philadelphia: Carey and Hart.

DAVIES, J.D. (1955). Phrenology, fad and science—A 19th century American crusade. New Haven, Conn.: Yale University Press.

DE GUISTINO, D. (1969). Phrenology in Britain, 1815-1855. University of Wisconsin: Ph.D. dissertation.

DE QUIROS, C.B. (1911). Modern theories of criminality. Boston: Little, Brown.

Encyclopedia Britannica (1911), 11th Edition. New York: University Press.

FINK, A.E. (1938). The causes of crime: Biological theories in the United States, 1800-1915. Philadelphia: University of Pennsylvania Press.

FOWLER, O.S. and FOWLER, L.N. (1834). Phrenology proved, illustrated and applied. Philadelphia: Fowler and Brevoort.

GALL, F.J. (1807). Craniologie ou Découvertes Nouvelles Concernment de Cerveau, le Crâne et les organes. Paris.

——— and SPURZHEIM, J.G. (1810-1819). Anatomie et Physiologie du System Nerveaux en General et du Cerveau en Particular. Avec des Observations Sur la Possibilité de Reconnoitre Plusiers. Dispositions Intellectuelles et Morales de L'Homme et des Animaux par la Configuration de Leur Tetes. [Volumes I-IV]. Paris.

GORING, C. (1913). The English Convict. London: His Majesty's Stationary Office.

JACOBS, G. (1971). "Phrenology—A scientific hydra." Unpublished paper.

KNOTT, J. (1906). "Franz Joseph Gall and the science of phrenology." Westminster Review, 166:150-163.

LANTERI, L. (1970). Historie de la Phrénologie. Paris: Presses Univeristaries de France.

MANNHEIM, H. (ed, 1960). Pioneers in criminology. Chicago: Quadrangle Press.

RIEGEI, R.E. (1933). "The Introduction of phrenology to the United States." American Historical Review, 39:73-78.

SAVITZ, L.D. (1972). "Introduction" to Lombroso-Ferrero, G., *Criminal Man* (reprinted). Montclair, N.J.: Patterson Smith.

SCHAFER, S. (1969). Theories in criminology. New York: Random House.

SEWELL, T. (1937). An examination of phrenology. Washington, D.C.: B. Homans.

STERN, M.B. (1971). Heads and headlines: The phrenological Fowlers. Norman: University of Oklahoma Press.

TEMKIN, O. (1947). "Gall and the phrenological movement." Bulletin of the History of Medicine, 21:275-321.

VOLD, G.B. (1958). Theoretical criminology. New York: Oxford University Press.

WATSON, H.C. (1830). Statistics of phrenology: Being a sketch of the progress and present state of that science in the British Islands. London.

Leonard J. Hippchen
*Virginia Commonwealth
University*

3

CONTRIBUTIONS OF
BIOCHEMICAL RESEARCH TO
CRIMINOLOGICAL THEORY

Findings from the great volume of research in biochemistry over the past two decades suggest the need to make important modifications in current criminological theory. It appears that our present emphasis on sociological and psychological factors as explanations for crime is too limited and that our theory needs to be amended to accommodate these new discoveries in biochemistry.

The concern with the importance of biochemical findings to criminological theory is part of a broader concern which social scientists have been expressing in recent years. A large number of investigators have described the neglect of the total spectrum of biological factors in the sociological and criminological literature (Shah and Roth, 1974; Meade and Parkes, 1965; Handler, 1970; Means, 1967; Eckland, 1967; van den Berghe, 1975; Wilson, 1975; Hinde, 1975; Figlio, 1976).

Shah and Roth, in particular, emphasize that the explosion of knowledge in experimental behavior genetics, human population genetics, the biochemistry of the nervous system, experimental and clinical endocrinology, and neurophysiology now permit fuller consideration of biological factors as contributing variables in the development of antisocial forms of behavior.

The essence of the findings in relation to the biochemistry of the nervous system is that behavior associated with delinquency and crime can be caused by chemical deficiencies or imbalances in the body or by brain toxicity. The purpose of this writing is to review the emerging theory and some of the basic research and applied applications which relate to this theory. A final section then will discuss some implications of these factors to the further development of our criminological thought.

A BIOCHEMICAL THEORY OF CRIME CAUSATION

Biochemical research has discovered that the functioning of the brain is affected by the molecular concentrations of many substances that are normally present in the brain. The optimum concentrations of these substances for a person may differ greatly from the concentrations provided by his normal diet and genetic machinery. Abnormal deficits or excesses in these molecular brain concentrations, depending upon the specific and varying individual needs of each person, can lead to a variety of pathological thought and behavior patterns and, under some conditions, may be seen as "antisocial."

This explanation of behavior, stemming from biochemical causes, was first given by Linus Pauling (1968), Nobel Prize recipient for his discoveries in biochemistry. He called it an "orthomolecular theory" of behavior. Although it is a general theory of optimal human functioning and dysfunctioning, the dysfunctions described are strikingly similar to behavior often labelled as "delinquent" or "criminal." Thus, these aspects of the theory appear to be important to criminologists.

Orthomolecular theory states that these chemical deficiencies or imbalances, or brain toxicities, can originate from genetic factors or they can be induced especially during the birth process or in early childhood by improper nutrition of the mother and/or child. This thesis has seen a relatively rapid development in the medical treatment of these biochemical dysfunctions, and many of these treatments have been extended to alcoholics, drug addicts, delinquents, and criminals. The Huxley Biosocial Research Institute, a national orthomolecular group, recently compiled a list of more than 400 such medical practitioners in the United States and Canada who are using the new biochemical therapies.

MAJOR GROUPINGS OF OBSERVED SYMPTOMS
AND THEIR TREATMENT

There are two major groupings of symptoms which may accompany biochemical deficiencies or abnormalities in the body, and which may be seen as "antisocial": (1) perceptual changes due to nutritional disorders or to brain allergy; and (2) hyperactivity due to nutritional deficiencies or to hypogly-cemia. These symptoms recently have been defined by Hoffer (1975), a leading figure in the orthomolecular movement.

Perceptual Changes

A broad group of perceptual changes can be caused either by vitamin deficiencies or by vitamin dependencies. If a person with a normal need for vitamins does not consume food which provides these needs, he will suffer from a vitamin *deficiency*. A person who has requirements for certain vitamins far in excess of the normal amounts may suffer from a vitamin deficiency even with a normal diet. This is called a vitamin *dependency*.

For example, research has shown that alcoholics develop an excessive need for thiamine. This is caused typically by their poor diets. If they are not given large doses of thiamine they may develop a very serious, deadly disease called Wernicke-Korsakoff. Or, a person may have an extremely high require-ment for the B-3 vitamin and on a normal diet he may develop pellegra. This is a vitamin dependency, probably due to a genetic or birth defect. Whereas the *deficiency* was produced by a poor diet for a person with normal needs, the *dependency* was produced by a normal diet for a person with abnormal needs for a specific vitamin.

A person with a vitamin deficiency-dependency disease can suffer severe distortions in seeing, hearing, and the other special senses. The person also can become very violent at times. The changes in perception can lead to behavior which can be identi-fied as antisocial or criminal. Usually the person involved or those around him do not understand the source of the behavior and they may impute erroneous motivations to this behavior. This can be true at the level of infant, child, youth, or adult.

A number of studies have found that these vitamin deficiencies-dependencies are common among criminal groups. Hoffer (1975) has reported that his studies found that 70% of the criminals charged with serious crimes had a B-6 dependency problem. He also found that a majority of the alcoholics and drug addicts studied were B-3 and B-6 dependents. Further, he has estimated that the majority of all acute and subacute schizophrenics and children with learning disabilities and behavior disorders are B-3 and B-6 dependents.

R.J. Green (in Brereton, 1975), a medical consultant at Saskatchewan Penitentiary in Prince Albert, Canada, also has reported that a majority of the inmates at that prison were suffering from some form of vitamin deficiency-dependency. Of the total prisoners examined, he found that one-third were suffering from perceptual distortions caused by a B-6 deficiency.

The second major cause of perceptual changes is food allergies. H.L. Newbold and his associates (1972) have found a large number of substances which in some persons can trigger violent allergic reactions. Perceptual distortions were found in his studies to be highest on a selected group of subjects for such foods as wheat, corn, and milk.

Green, in his study of Saskatchewan inmates, found that at least one-third of the prisoners also had "proprioceptive dysperception," meaning that their brains misled them into thinking they suffered from such problems as duodenal ulcer, heart pain, and arthritis. These persons, Green says, are affected by allergies which disturb the central nervous system. Typically these persons are classified as neurotics or paranoid psychopaths, but, Green states, these are not treatable entities as are allergies.

A number of medical practitioners have reported striking results in use of orthomolecular approaches to treatment of crime-related types of behavior. The typical therapy involves use of the identified deficient-dependent vitamins in megadoses. For example, Russell E. Smith (1974), a physician at Brighton Hospital in Detroit, Michigan, treated 507 hard-core alcoholics to massive doses (3 to 5 grams daily) of vitamin B-3. The project covered a two-year period, 1967-1968, and the follow-up of these patients showed a recovery rate (sobriety) of 71%.

Vic Pawlak (1972), director of a drug center in Phoenix, Arizona, has reported excellent results in dealing with drug problems with use of 3 grams daily of vitamins B-3 and C. He states that his center began using this form of treatment when it was observed that hard-core drug users have a set of symptoms almost identical to those of schizophrenia. Since this treatment had proved to be 80% successful in treatment of schizophrenia, they adopted this approach several years ago with immediate and dramatic results. They claim over the past four years 80% success both with drug users and alcoholics at their center. David Hawkins (1972), director of the North Nassau Mental Health Clinic in Long Island, New York, has reported extensive use of megavitamin therapy with outstanding success in treatment of alcoholics, suicides, drug addicts, and schizophrenics. The clinic treats an average of 1,500 outpatients annually, and they have treated more than 7,000 persons using this method. They claim an average 75% recovery rate.

Abram Hoffer and Humphrey Osmond of Canada (Cott, 1972) were the first in 1952 to use massive doses of vitamin B-3 in the treatment of schizophrenia. They achieved 80% in complete and permanent remission of all symptoms as long as their patients were maintained on 3 grams daily doses. Later they added vitamins B-6, C, E, and several other vitamins and minerals to their research studies and showed even greater success.

F.C. Dohan and J.C. Grasberger (1973), psychiatrists at mental hospitals in Pennsylvania, recently reported that schizophrenics who were assigned diets free of cereal grains and milk while on locked wards were discharged about twice as rapidly as control patients on high-cereal diets. The treatment in this study, as is typical of most brain allergy cases, is withdrawal of the allergic food or substance. Similar results in treatment of brain allergies have been reported by William Philpott (1974), psychiatrist at Fuller Memorial Sanitarium in Massachusetts, and Marshall Mandell (in Newbold et al., 1972), director, New England Foundation for Allergies and Environmental Diseases in Norwalk, Conn.

Allan Cott (1972), a private physician in New York City, has reported successfully treating more than 500 children with learning disabilities and behavioral disturbances with vitamins B-3, B-6, C, and E. Bernard Rimland (1974), director of the Institute for Child Behavior Research of San Diego, also has been working with a large group of children who experienced learning and/or behavioral problems in schools, and he has reported excellent results to date in an on-going study in use of massive doses of vitamins B-3 and B-6.

Hyperactivity

Hyperactivity frequently is interpreted as an "antisocial" form of behavior. But it may be caused either by nutritional deficiencies or by a condition of low blood sugar (hypoglycemia). Nutritionists relate this symptom as resulting from consumption of products containing large quantities of refined sugars and starches and to quantities of food additives. This eating pattern can produce a reaction in the body in which now and then there are major fluctuations in the blood sugar levels.

Medical experts in the field testify to the fact that this condition can have an amazing effect on behavior, in some cases producing symptoms of lethargy and depression, and in other cases irritability, suspiciousness, bizarre thoughts, hallucinations, extreme mania, anxiety, and violent behavior. Joseph Wilder (1947) conducted a study of juvenile delinquents and criminals and concluded that most were suffering from hypoglycemia, but that they had been arrested for a variety of offenses: disorderly conduct, assault and battery, attempted suicide and homicide, cruelty against children or spouse, sexual perversions and aggressions, false fire alarms, drunkenness, embezzlement, petty larceny, willful destruction of property, arson, slander, and violation of traffic regulations.

An overactive child is too distractable, too restless to learn or to respond appropriately to cues for social learning. Thus, the overactive child easily can be labelled a "problem" child by parents and teachers, and early made to feel rejected or as a misfit in society. Many of these children, because they are unable to learn, can grow into adulthood with a wide variety of deficiencies in knowledge and skills. They also are prime candidates as truants and school dropouts, and they may become delinquents and criminals.

Abram Hoffer has studied more than 400 children over the past 15 years who exhibited a wide variety of learning and behavioral disorders, hyperactivity being one of the most common symptoms. Hoffer found that a large proportion of the children were vitamin B-3 dependent. If not treated early, Hoffer predicted that these children would develop a variety of schizophrenic symptoms before they are 25 years old. He attributes this condition of B-3 dependency as the primary cause of restlessness among the youth today, leading them to such activity as smoking, alcohol, drugs, running away, truancy, vandalism, violence, and delinquency and crime.

Hoffer has estimated that about 90% of the criminal homicides found in prisons, diagnosed as paranoid schizophrenics, are in reality suffering from hypoglycemia or some vitamin deficiency. Hoffer also states that alcohol is another addiction which is a high breeder of crime, and that alcoholics tend to be sugar addicts as well and thus hypoglycemic. He says that he has tested several hundred alcoholics and that he has yet to find one who did not suffer from *relative* hypoglycemia—the degree of this disorder most likely to show itself in violent behavior. It is subclinical; it is not easy to detect except by specially developed diagnostic testing. Drug addicts also have been found to evidence a high degree of hypoglycemia.

D'Asaro (1973), in conducting a study of inmates in the Morris County (New Jersey) jail, concluded that inmates consume significantly more sugar, alcohol, and caffein than noninmates, and related this finding to the high degree of restlessness in the prison. Correction of this problem through proper dietary means significantly reduced the amount of disciplinary reports and improved the inmates' functioning in academic and vocation classes.

J.A. Yaryura-Tobias (1975), research director of the North Nassau Mental Health Clinic in Manhasset, New York, also recently has published a summary of findings relating violent behavior to hypoglycemia.

Hypoglycemia typically is treated with a combination high protein, low carbohydrate diet, and multivitamin therapy. Hoffer has treated numerous cases of hypoglycemia successfully using the high protein diet, eliminating sugars and starches, and with large doses of vitamins B-3, B-6, C, and E.

R.J. Green, in his treatment of inmates at the Saskatchewan Penitentiary in Canada, recommended a four-day rotational diet, high in protein and curtailing sweets, sparing use of coffee, tea, cocoa, pop, and other stimulants—if at all, smoking restricted to certain areas and at certain times, physical exercise, and megavitamins as required.

IMPLICATIONS OF BIOCHEMICAL RESEARCH AND THERAPY FOR CRIMINOLOGICAL THEORY

The intention of this brief review of biochemical research and therapy has been to alert the community of criminologists to what appears to be important new knowledge. Shah and Roth (1974) and Figlio (1976) also have pointed to this new knowledge and of its importance to our understanding of antisocial behavior. Figlio, in his review of the empirical support for biological aspects of criminal behavior, concluded that the most convincing data was in the area of biochemical factors.

It is clear that most of the research in biology has not been originated by criminologists. Criminologists in recent years have tended to come primarily from the sociological or psychological branches of science. Thus, it is not likely that they would have hit upon biochemical or other biological factors in their search for the causes of crime.

Shah and Roth (1974) suggest that social scientists have failed to investigate seriously the contributions of biology because they have become bound-up in the nature-nurture controversy. It is assumed that a "cause" must either be biological *or* environmental, and social scientists tend to identify strongly with the environmental position. The facts of the matter today, however, suggest that causation is not an either-or proposition, but rather that a wide variety of biological, psychological, and sociological factors are in a continuous process of interaction and process unfoldment.

It is interesting to note that the original basic research which has led to development of the orthomolecular theory was far removed in thought and intent from the criminal field. The earliest of these biochemical researchers appear to have been interested in the relation of vitamins and minerals to physical health. Later, they began to correlate their research findings with certain mental symptoms, such as neuroticism and psychosis. Still later they became interested in genetic and birth defects and related childhood disorders.

Up to the present time, only a limited amount of research and applied practice has been instituted directly with delinquents and criminals, but a start has been made. The findings to this time suggest that the biochemical aspects of juvenile delinquency and crime are *real*. They appear to be even more valid in the areas of child behavioral problems in the home and school, for poor performance and dropouts in the school, for truancy and vandalism, for early sex problems, for violence, and for alcohol and narcotic abuse among our youth. These conditions have been shown to correlate highly with delinquency and crime (Wacker, 1974).

Obviously, much more research is needed to quantify much more precisely the role and extent of biochemical factors in delinquency and crime. The data to this time, however, should stimulate criminologists to further test and validate the orthomolecular theory.

Whereas in the past the role of biological factors in crime largely has been rejected by criminologists, it now appears to be time to work out a new partnership with the orthomolecular researcher and practitioner and to "team research" this new area of biochemical knowledge. Criminological theory then, it is felt, will be greatly strengthened: the new theory, in my view, will need to be more balanced to account both for biochemical and psychosocial factors in the development of "antisocial" forms of behavior. This knowledge also can be used to strengthen the applied area of correction which today is under attack and is in need of more effective correctional tools.

REFERENCES

BRERETON, L. (1975). "Subclinical pellegra among penitentiary inmates." Humanist in Canada, 8(September):10-11.

CLEMENTS, S.D., and LINDSLEY, D.B. (eds., (1967). Brain function agression and defense: Neural mechanisms and social patterns (Vol. 5). Berkeley: University of California Press.

COTT, A. (1972). "Orthomolecular treatment: A biochemical approach to treatment of schizophrenia." New York: American Schizophrenia Foundation reprint.

D'ASARO, B. (1973). "Dietary habits of jail inmates." Report of the Morris County Jail Rehabilitation Program. Morristown, N.J.: Office of the Sheriff.

DOHAN, F.C., and GRASBERGER, J.C. (1973). "Relapsed schizophrenias earlier discharged from the hospital after cereal-free, milk-free diet." American Journal of Psychiatry, 130(June):206-221.

ECKLAND, B.K. (1967). "Genetics and sociology: A reconsideration." American Sociological Review, 32:173-194.

EICKENWALD, H.F., and FRY, P.C. (1969). "Nutrition and learning." Science, 163(February):644-648.

FIGLIO, R.M. (1976). "The biological basis of criminal behavior: A critique." Presented at the 1976 annual meeting of the American Society of Criminology.

GARATTINI, S., and SIGGS, E.B. (eds., 1969). Agressive Behavior. New York: John Wiley.

HANDLER, P. (ed., 1970). Biology and the future of man. New York: Oxford University Press.

HAWKINS, D.R. (1973). "The development of an integrated community system for effective treatment of schizophrenia." In D. Hawkins and L. Pauling (eds.), Orthomolecular psychiatry: Treatment of schizophrenia. New York: W.H. Freeman.

HESTON, L.J. (1970). "The genetics of schizophrenia and schizoid disease." Science, 164(January):249-256.

HINDE, R.A. (1975). Biological basis of human behavior. New York: McGraw-Hill.

HOFFER, A. (1975). "The relation of crime to nutrition." Humanist in Canada, 8(September):2-9.

McCLEARN, G.E. (1969). "Biological bases of social behavior with special reference to violent behavior." Pp. 979-1017 in D.J. Mulvihill, Crimes of Violence (Vol. 13). Washington, D.C.: U.S. Government Printing Office.

MEADE, J.E., and PARKES, A.S. (eds., 1965). Biological aspects of social problems. New York: Plenum Press.

MEANS, R.L. (1967). "Sociology, biology and the analysis of social problems." Social Problems, 15:200-212.

NEWBOLD, H.L., et al. (1972). "Psychiatric syndromes produced by allergies: Ecological mental illness." Presented at the 1972 annual meeting of the Academy of Orthomolecular psychiatry.

PAULING, L. (1968). "Orthomolecular psychiatry." Science, 160(April):265-271.

PAWLAK, V. (1972). "Megavitamin therapy and the drug wipeout syndrome." Phoenix, Ariz.: Do It Now Foundation, Inc., reprint.

PHILPOTT, W.H. (1974). "Ecologic, orthomolecular, and behavioral contributions to psychiatry." Journal of Orthomolecular Psychiatry, 3(November):356-370.

RIMLAND, B. (1974). "An orthomolecular study of psychotic children." Journal of Orthomolecular Psychiatry, 3(November):371-377.

SHAH, S.A., and ROTH, L.H. (1974). "Biological and psychophysiological factors in criminality." Pp. 101-173 in D. Glaser, (ed.), Handbook of criminology. Chicago: Rand McNally.

SMITH, R.F. (1974). "A five-year field trial of massive nicotinic and therapy of alcoholics in Michigan." Journal of Orthomolecular Psychiatry, 3(October): 327-331.

Van den BERGHE, P.L. (1975). Man in society. New York: Elsevier.

WACKER, J.A. (1974). "The reduction of crime through the prevention and treatment of learning disabilities." A Report to the Law Enforcement Assistance Administration. Dallas: Wacker Corporation.

WILSON, E.O. (1975). Sociobiology: The new synthesis. Cambridge, Mass.: Belknap.

YARYURA-TOBIAS, J.A. (1975). "Violent behavior, brain dysrhythma and glucose dysfunction: A new syndrome." Journal of Orthomolecular Psychiatry, 4(October):182-188.

Harold E. Pepinsky
Indiana University

4

THE ROOM FOR DESPOTISM IN THE QUEST FOR VALID CRIME STATISTICS
American Crime Measurement in Historical and Comparative Perspective

Not so long ago in the United States, it was commonly accepted that officials of state could respond to a crime only after someone had been found guilty of the crime (beyond a reasonable doubt) by a judge or jury. This was a necessary condition for establishing that a crime had in fact occurred. As of today, as a pretext for official action, we have moved far in the direction of giving mere residents of our communities the authority to establish that a crime has in fact occurred merely by reporting it anonymously to a private interviewer. Crime rates as reported by self-declared victims are as much as ten times as great as those reported by police (Reynolds, 1972), and in the Federal Bureau of Investigation's (1975: 11, 176) national statistics for what they call "index offenses," the police crime rates are nearly fourteen times the size of the conviction rates. By the most advanced current standards, there is estimated to be more than one hundred times as much crime as there would be by application of a 19th century standard.

At first one had to be a judge or juror to have authority in decisions as to what to add to crime statistics, later a police officer, and then a member of any household throughout a

AUTHOR'S NOTE: Special thanks for constructive criticism go to Ellen Dwyer, Ted Ferdinand, and Barton Parks.

community. The authority to define sizes and trends in our crime problem has been diffused among Americans, as victim survey results have risen to political preeminence as indicators of how much criminal justice protection our citizens need. Far from discouraging our citizens from calling on the state's resources to intervene in interpersonal conflict, we are strengthening the presumption that simple, uncorroborated allegations of citizens are by themselves proof that crimes have occurred. It can be said that this represents a democratization of the finding of crime.

There has not been a concomitant democratization of the response to crime. Indeed, it is common for citizens to be warned not to "take the law into their own hands." Herein lies a partial fulfillment of a prophecy, made by Tocqueville (1956:301-314) in the middle of the 19th century, of a growth of a certain type of despotism in the course of development of American democracy. Tocqueville foresaw the danger that citizens would become so preoccupied with personal material gain that they would turn over to various officials of state as much responsibility as they could for management of their relations with others. What Tocqueville failed to foresee was a changing role for the judiciary. In his time, the judiciary was primarily seen as a restraining force on usurpations of individual rights by other officials. However, in this century, the courts and, in the criminal justice system, associated agencies, from the police to correctional agencies, have tried increasingly to act as parents to their child-citizens, using the law as a pretext to manage the lives of ever larger portions of the populace. It appears that the quest for valid crime statistics has been tied symbiotically to this development. It is the thesis of this paper that we are confronted with a choice of trade-offs: either (a) we continue to enlarge the authority of the general populace to find crimes while restricting their authority to manage interpersonal conflicts privately; or (b) we move to restrict the authority of the general populace to demand state criminal justice system protection while enlarging their authority to manage their conflicts privately. The more criminal justice protection belongs to the people, the less people's day-to-day relations with others belong to themselves. If criminal justice officials become despots by refusing to recognize the legitimacy of people's calls for assistance, they also become despots by easing the restraint with which they recognize those calls. Implicit in the quest for valid crime statistics is a dilemma: as we pursue a form of democracy, we encounter a corollary form of despotism.

A HISTORICAL REVIEW
OF AMERICAN CRIME MEASUREMENT

Elsewhere (1976c), this author has reviewed the history of American crime measurement in detail, and has argued that the growth of crime in the United States can be accounted for as the outcome of a self-fulfilling prophecy of American crime measurement specialists—a prophecy resting on the assumptions that crime rates are always underreported rather than overreported, and that crime rates generally increase. The reader is referred there for the historical detail; the historical review here is more brief and general.

A concept central to the development of estimates of crime rates has been that of "the dark figure." This refers to the crime hidden from those who gather crime statistics, which thus does not appear in the numerators of crime rate figures. The dark figure has been an obsession in American crime measurement since the beginning of this century. In the first major scholarly study of crime measurement in the United States, Robinson (1911) argued that the "main difference" between prison and judicial statistics—the two kinds of crime statistics that had been gathered by a growing number of states since the Jacksonian era—was that judicial statistics were the "far more complete" of the two. Moreover, he criticized even judicial statistics as being deficient. His critique reflected the growing popularity among local jurisdictions of collecting arrest statistics as crime measures, although arrest statistics had earlier been occasionally used for political purposes. Inciardi (1976:179-180) has found an account of use of arrest figures to support police budgetary demands in New York City as early as 1858 (Costello, 1885). Before arrest figures became established as an indicator of sizes and trends in the crime problem, a mandate was given to the Federal Bureau of Investigation, in 1930, to collect the first nationwide crime statistics, using a measure called "offenses known to the police" (National Commission on Law Ovservance and Enforcement, 1931). As matters now stand, the convention is that an offense is known to the police if a police officer files a report to that effect, a report generally based on a citizen complaint. Detectives can "unfound" an offense report, which on a national average they do to 4% of reports (FBI, 1976:10). Police department and FBI analysts (President's Commission on Law Enforcement and Administration of Justice, 1967b:211) sometimes adjust offenses known rate figures when they are much different from what is expected, but an offense is never unfounded in light of later court proceedings such as a not guilty verdict.

Since the rise of offenses known data, a variety of other techniques has been used to expand the scope of the crime problem. Among them have been a movement to locate more white-collar crime and the use of self-report questionnaires to ask respondents, usually children, how many offenses they themselves have committed. The one new data collection technique that has been widely used to estimate crime rates is the victim survey. This technique was first developed in three studies commissioned by the President's Commission on Law Enforcement and Administration of Justice (1967a). Victim surveys have since proliferated as a means to establishing "true," "real," or "actual" crime rates as closely as possible (i.e., to minimize the dark figure). As mentioned earlier, up to ten times the offenses known crime rates have been found by this technique.

In the typical victim survey, a random sample of households is interviewed in one or more communities. Respondents are asked if members of their households have been the victims of one or more of a list of offenses during the preceding year. Affirmative responses are followed up in detail. Attempts may be made to validate the data obtained in any one of a variety of ways, as by rejecting data the interviewers feel are unreliable and by having legal experts check the offense descriptions in the interview protocols, but few victim reports are invalidated by such procedures. True to American tradition, a recent article, arguing that there is a serious risk of overreporting by the latest crime measurement method, stands in splendid isolation (Levine, 1976). Instead, there has been concern that crime rates might be substantially underreported in victim survey data. For instance, in one of the original victimization studies, Reiss (1967:150) interviewed a sample of persons who had reported offenses to the police in Detroit during the preceding month, and found that 20% of these offenses went unreported in the victim survey interviews. Reiss concluded that this was evidence of underreporting in the victim survey, though it would have been no less logical to conclude that police figures uncorroborated by the victim survey were overreported.

From a strictly methodological standpoint, two interpretations of the inflation of American crime rates are equally tenable. One interpretation is that Americans have characteristically hidden crime from public view. This has been the standard interpretation in American crime measurement literature. The other interpretation is that Americans, with the assistance of measurers of crime, have shown an increasing propensity to inflate the incidence of crime. Though the issue of choice of interpretation is not subject to scientific debate, it is subject to political debate. The choice of interpretation can be argued in terms of its political ramifications. One set of political ramifications arises from the relationship between the finding of crime (by crime measurement) and the response to crime (through criminal justice processes). To this end, the growth of crime measurement may be related to the development of criminal justice processes in the United States.

RESPONSE TO CRIME

Rothman has done extensive research on the growth of response to crime in the United States. In the 19th century, he has found a steady growth of total institutions, notably including prisons, for confining people (Rothman, 1971). He traces this growth to increased geographical mobility and community breakdown in the Jacksonian era. Rationalized as a humanitarian movement to avoid the horrors of capital and corporal punishment, the growth of these institutions has been found by Rothman to have had the effect of increasing both the length of state sanctions imposed in response to crime, and the proportion of the populace subjected to criminal sanction. At the front end of the criminal justice system, the 19th century also saw the growth in the number and size of police forces. As noted above, higher arrest figures produced by the police had become a pretext for the growth of police forces as early as the mid-19th century. As Rothman shows, periodic disenchantment with the effectiveness of official measures to control crime and criminals generally resulted in the elaboration and growth, not the simplification and decline, of official crime control measures.

Rothman has carried his research into the 20th century, and is in the process of writing up findings on the effects of introduction of new crime control measures at the beginning of this century (for a preliminary report, see Rothman, 1975). In the guise of diversion of persons from the criminal justice process, the range of these measures included probation, parole, and the juvenile or family court. Rothman has found that these measures have had practically no effect on the rate at which people have been incarcerated, and have served instead to place new quotas of persons under state supervision for criminal behavior.

The growth of response to crime in the United States can be accounted for as an interaction of the breakdown of interpersonal trust among the general populace and the growth of criminal justice bureaucracy (Pepinsky, 1976a). Americans have concentrated on developing institutions which facilitate termination of interpersonal relationships as a response to interpersonal conflict. Divorce has been made easier. The development of transport technology has made it easier to move people and goods to greater distances and with greater ease, reinforcing people's tendencies simply to move away from interpersonal conflicts. The development of communications technology has made it easier for people to find new places to work and to live. And for those who prefer not to use these facilities to move away from conflict, a proliferation of conflict managers has made it easier to have troublesome others moved instead. One set of channels for having others moved lies in what is loosely known as the criminal justice system. For instance, where once a neighborhood child's throwing a stone through a window might have been seen as a matter for private discussion with the child's parents, it has been observed by this writer to be a common type of incident for referral to the police (Pepinsky, 1976b).

In general, the American response to the perception that the crime problem is growing has been one of increased reliance on a growing criminal justice bureaucracy to arbitrate conflict. At the national level, economic support for this response has come to be practically monopolized by the Law Enforcement Assistance Adminsitration in the United States Department of Justice, which has been given resources primarily for the development of official technology and facilities and the growth of official manpower as a strategy of crime control. The official growth function has its limits, to be sure. For example, police have had trouble maintaining rates at which they clear offenses known to them by arrest, let alone increasing these clearance rates (though arrest rates themselves have generally shown persistent increases). But if one looks at the probability that an American will be subject to criminal justice jurisdiction as an alleged criminal offender, that probability has rather steadily increased at least since the Jacksonian period. More and more, Americans have proven unable or unwilling to manage their day-to-day interpersonal affairs without official criminal justice intervention.

If the defining principle of democracy is that citizens shall govern their own affairs, this trend in response to crime literally represents a kind of decline in the level of democracy in the United States. It appears that the relationship between the undemocratization of response to conflict and the democratization of the finding of crime is symbiotic. Tappan (1947) came close to describing this relationship in the course of his attack on Sutherland (1940) for proposing to democratize the definition of crime. As the finding of crime has become democratized, crime has been found to be an increasingly pervasive feature of American social life. With this, the threshold at which people call on criminal justice officials to take over their affairs has been lowered, and the pretext for increasing the proportion of the populace employed as criminal justice officials has been strengthened. More officials and a lower threshold for referring problems to officials has facilitated official demonstrations that there is more crime than ever to be managed. This has generated support for efforts to devise techniques to find more of what once would have been "hidden" crime. And so the cycle goes. The twin processes of democratization and of its antithesis support and feed one another. Americans are being given increasing power to relinquish control over their relations with one another, and they are putting the power to its use. This is one of the central dilemmas of social control policy in the United States in our time—one that has scarcely been addressed, let alone resolved.

COMPARATIVE PERSPECTIVE

In practically any political order one could imagine, the capacity of persons to manage their own interpersonal conflicts would be seen as necessary to the survival of the current regime. A political order can perhaps be stable and autocratic in many respects, but political stability requires respect for democracy in the realm of interpersonal conflict management. Perhaps nowhere has this been more thoughtfully articulated than in China, where representatives of one culture have worked steadily at defining the role of crime in political theory for at least a couple of millenia. By the time of the last imperial dynasty (the Manchu or Ch'ing, 1644-1911), the Chinese had come to recognize that the emperor's hegemony depended on people's being able to manage their own conflicts without resort to official intervention. (For detailed descriptions of law in Manchu China, see Bodde and Morris, 1967, and Van der Sprenkel, 1962). If magistrates had to take cognizance of too much crime, it was a sign of a breakdown in the social order that ultimately would result in the emperor's loss of his "mandate of heaven."

Imperial hegemony rested in large part on the strength of private governance of interpersonal affairs, and the growth of criminal case loads represented a failure of this governance in particular and of governance in general.

This was one aspect of recognition of the Confucian expression of the natural law of social order. Another aspect was that, when the emperor or his representatives acted to manage interpersonal conflict, any punishment that was imposed on an offender had to be made to fit the crime. If officials did not impose proper punishments, this, too, would indicate that the emperor has lost his grip on his naturally given role in the social order, and stood to lose his mandate. Hence, elaborate criminal codes were written to indicate which sanction to attach to a crime, and Boards of Punishment routinely reviewed the sanctions imposed by magistrates to scrutinize their legality. A magistrate who recognized a citizen complaint of a crime and did not thereafter impose a punishment was liable to punishment himself. One avenue open to the magistrate was to obtain a confession of having made a false complaint from the complainant (by torture if necessary), and then to resolve the case by punishing the complainant. If the magistrate was found by a Board of Punishments to have imposed an improper punishment, he was to suffer the punishment himself (or a punishment one degree lower if the punishment had been set but not imposed). Understandably, citizens were reluctant to lodge complaints and officials were reluctant to accept them. People scarcely relied on the services of lawyers, who were affectionately known as "litigation tricksters." It was in the interest of officials and of citizens alike to see that as many disputes and conflicts as possible were handled within the structure of families, of clans, and of guilds.

For conflicts that transcended family, clan, or group lines, the institution of mediation became highly ritualized and developed. With the help of mediators, who carried information back and forth and proposed terms of dispute settlement, many conflicting parties who had not simply let matters drop were brought together in ceremonies of agreement to terms of settlement of their differences.

This tradition of mediation and avoidance of resort to law has been carried over into the People's Republic of China. Today in China, there is no criminal or civil code—just a few short statutes. By all accounts—by the Chinese themselves, by refugees, and by visitors who have included many born and raised in China—arrests, trials, incarceration, and execution have become rare events. In the last 15 years, with alternate periods of emphasis, conflict has been channeled into the intergroup or faction level on the one hand and the level of work groups, residence groups, and production brigades (where "criticism and struggle" is a recurrent ritual)—with the services of mediators made available—on the other. It is characteristic of this structure that a judge may go to a work group and mediate a dispute there instead of holding court (Lubman, 1973). Attempts have been made to undermine the hierarchical foundation of traditional social organization by placing people in newly created groups, but the traditional resistance to use of law has been carried over from the past.

The dynastic Chinese were elaborate record keepers, but the data they recorded about crime were designed to give exemplars of how cases should be decided rather than to give quantitative measures of criminal behavior. This is similar to the development of case law records in Europe and in the United States. This kind of data is intended for use primarily by officers of the court to guide and control their decision-making. China and the West have diverged in the kind of social conflict data that had been developed for others than practitioners of law. In China, the development is recent, in part because few Chinese other than officials could read until recently. There, as in newspapers, descriptions of group sessions, including sessions devoted to responding to conflict, appear as exemplars of how conflict should be generated and managed extralegally. Like case law for judges, this information about domestic conflict is intended as a model for attempts at conflict resolution.

The American counterpart has been represented in crime statistics: the development of descriptions of conflict behavior rather than the development of descriptions of ways people can try to work through conflicts to which they are parties. From

European antecedents in the utilitarianism of Bentham and Beccaria and in the moral calculus of Guerry and Quetelet, Americans have invested themselves in providing information to substantiate the case that parties to conflict are incapable of adequate response themselves and must rely instead on the services of experts trained in scientific application of principles of utilitarian rationality. At the most sophisticated level of extralegal conflict information, the quest for valid crime statistics, indicating that the crime problem is far bigger than we had imagined and is still growing, lends credence to other kinds of information such as fictionalized television accounts of how the police constantly save Americans from the sad fate of having to deal with one another without official oversight.

The Chinese experience indicates that high and growing crime rates, and heavy reliance on criminal justice processes for response to interpersonal conflict, are not inevitable features of life in a large, complex polity. By comparison to Americans, the Chinese are far less democratic about empowering people to find crime, but far more democratic about empowering people to respond to their own conflicts with others without official intervention. The Chinese offer Americans an empirical referent for the direction that might be taken by changing the course of American attempts to democratize social control. Control over the finding of crime has been diffused in the United States, while control over response to interpersonal conflict has been centralized. By centralizing control over the finding of crime and diffusing control over response to interpersonal conflict, we would be introducing another area for the growth of despotism while we strengthened a form of democracy. In the process, the quest for valid crime statistics might give way to the quest for information about how people in private settings addressed themselves to interpersonal conflict. In part, Tocqueville's prophecy has been fulfilled. We have fostered the growth of a kind of despotism in America, and the quest for valid crime statistics has played a role in that growth. However, it would be a mistake to conclude that reversal of the trend would imply an absolute reduction in the level of despotism in American society. If we gain any freedom from placing American crime measurement in historical and comparative perspective, it is in part the freedom to choose among forms of despotism, not to oppose despotism altogether.

What trade-offs are implicit in this choice? Implicit in the choice of empowering people to find crime versus empowering people to respond to interpersonal conflict are:

1. The loss of official protection versus the loss of protection from friends, relatives, neighbors, and any other private person who might be in a physical position to give protection as needed.

2. Vulnerability to official cruelty versus vulnerability to official attention. By American standards, the torture and corporal punishment typical of dynastic Chinese criminal justice, and the summary executions and liquidation that periodically occurs in modern China, would be unconscionable. So would apparent Chinese indifference to rights of the accused. In contrast, Americans have become second-to-none in the proportion of their own population made subject to criminal justice jurisdiction. For instance, our incarceration rate is one of the highest in the world (Waller and Chan, 1974). The more harshly the political order is prepared to treat its suspects and convicts, the less prepared it is to treat anyone at all and vice versa.

3. Vulnerability to personal indifference versus vulnerability to personal officiousness. In contrast to the striking propensity of Americans to ignore others in distress (Latane, 1970), a Chinese person's family, work group, residence group, or production brigade will go to extraordinary lengths, recognizing no claims of personal privacy, to "help" integrate the person solidly into the group support system (Li, 1973).

The list could continue indefinitely. The political issues posed by the American quest for valid crime statistics are not of pure good versus pure bad, but of choosing which set of gains is preferable in light of attendant costs. For now, it suffices to note that the American quest for valid crime statistics is not the absolute good it has generally been assumed to be—that granting the premise that this quest increases the democratic power of a people in one respect, a decrease in that people's democratic power is implied in another. Americans may yet find the net price worth paying, but it does indeed appear that there is room for despotism in the quest for valid crime statistics.

REFERENCES

BODDE, D., and MORRIS, C. (1967). Law in Imperial China. Cambridge, Mass.: Harvard University Press.

COSTELLO, A.E. (1885). Our police protectors: History of the New York Police from the earliest period to the present time. New York: Author's Edition.

Federal Bureau of Investigation (1976). Crime in the United States: Uniform crime reports—1975. Washington, D.C.: U.S. Government Printing Office.

INCIARDI, J.A. (1976). "The role of criminal statistics and victim survey research in planning and organizing for more effective law enforcement." Pp. 177-189 in E.C. Viano (ed.), Victims and society. Washington, D.C.: Visage Press.

LATANE, B. (1970). Unresponsive bystander: Why doesn't he help? Englewood Cliffs, N.J.: Prentice-Hall.

LEVINE, D.P. (1976). "The potential for overreporting in criminal victimization surveys." Criminology, 14(November):307-330.

LI, V.H. (1973). "Law and penology: Systems of reform and correciton." Pp. 144-156, in M. Oksenberg (ed.), China's developmental experience. New York: Praeger.

LUBMAN, S. (1973). "A divorce trial—Peking style." Wall Street Journal (June 5).

National Commission on Law Observance and Enforcement (Wickersham Commission, 1931). No. 3: Report on criminal statistics. Washington, D.C.: U.S. Government Printing Office.

PEPINSKY, H.E. (1976a). Crime and conflict: A study of law and society. New York: Academic Press.

——— (1976b). "Police offense-reporting behavior." Journal of Research in Crime and Delinquency, 13(January):33-47.

——— (1976c). "The growth of crime in the United States." Annals of the American Academy of Political and Social Science, 423(January):23-30.

President's Commission on Law Enforcement and Administration of Justice (1967a). Field surveys. Washington, D.C.: U.S. Government Printing Office.

——— (1967b). Task Force report: Assessment of crime. Washington, D.C.: U.S. Government Printing Office.

REISS, A.J., Jr. (1967). "Measurement of the nature and amount of crime." In President's Commission on Law Enforcement and Administration of Justice, Field Surveys III: Studies in crime and law enforcement in major metropolitan areas. Washington, D.C.: U.S. Government Printing Office.

REYNOLDS, P.D. (1972). Victimization of the residents and their perceptions of community services—1971. Minneapolis, Minn.: Metropolitan Council of the Twin Cities.

ROBINSON, L.N. (1911). History and organization of criminal statistics in the United States. Boston: Houghton-Mifflin.

ROTHMAN, D.J. (1971). The discovery of the asylum: Social order and disorder in the new republic. Boston: Little, Brown.

——— (1975). "Behavior modification in total institutions. Hastings Center Report, 5(February):17-24.

SUTHERLAND, E.H. (1940). "White-collar criminality." American Sociological Review, 5(February):1-12.

TAPPAN, P.W. (1947). "Who is the criminal?" American Sociological Review, 12(February):96-102.

TOCQUEVILLE, A. de (R.D. Heffner, ed., 1956). Democracy in America. New York: New American Library.

Van der Sprenkel, S. (1962). Legal institutions in Manchu China. London: Athlone Press.

WALLER, I. and CHAN, J. (1974). "Prison use: A Canadian and international comparison." Criminal Law Quarterly, 17(December):47-71.

Joan McCord
Drexel University

5

A COMPARATIVE STUDY OF TWO GENERATIONS OF NATIVE AMERICANS

Three separate, but related, issues can be illuminated through studying criminal patterns of fathers and sons. One of these issues is the relationship between fathers' and sons' criminal behavior. Prior research has indicated that criminals have greater than chance probability of having criminal fathers (Farrington, 1973; Glueck and Glueck, 1950; J. McCord et al., 1963; McCord and McCord, 1959, 1960; Robins, 1966). Yet little is known about crime-specific relationships between fathers' and sons' crimes.

A second issue is that of changes in crime rates attributable to increased or decreased lawlessness. Reviewing the history of criminal statistics from 1829 to 1908, Robinson (1911) found that the period was marked largely by inadequate data collections (with the exception of Massachusetts' reports on prisoners). Continuing the history of criminal statistics to the period 1908 to 1933, Robinson (1933) reported progress in techniques for collecting and analyzing data and noted optimistically possible future growth in knowledge through Uniform Crime Reports.

AUTHOR'S NOTE: This research has been generously supported by PHS Research Grant no. 5 R01 MH26779, NIMH (Center for Studies of Crime and Delinquency), and has been conducted jointly with the Department of Probation of the Commonwealth of Massachusetts.

Uniform Crime Reports were first published in 1930. Despite their frequent use as a basis for judging changes in criminal behavior, these reports fail to take into account changes in age distributions and populations, descriptions of crimes, attitudes toward reporting criminal acts, and police behavior. (See Bell, 1960; Chilton and Spielberger, 1971; Ferdinand, 1970; Kitsuse and Cicourel, 1963; Pepinsky, 1976; Quinney, 1971; Sutherland and Cressey, 1974.)

A few studies trace crime rates prior to 1930. Lane (1976) reported decreasing criminal violence during America's first hundred years—attributing this to greater acceptance of routine brought about through institutionalization of conflict (in organized political parties), education, and industrialization. Ferdinand (1967) studied crime in Boston between 1849 and 1951. He found overall declines in major crimes. Only forcible rape showed a tendency toward increase; murder, larceny, and assault clearly declined. Willbach (1938) detected decreasing crimes of violence in New York City between 1916 and 1936.

Since previous analyses of crime are based on number of crimes reported—rather than number of criminals—they cannot be used as an adequate measure of spreading or shrinking lawlessness. Many crimes go unreported and reported crimes are partly a function of public attitudes (see Black, 1970; Erickson and Empey, 1963; Gold, 1966; Murphey et al., 1946; Porterfield, 1943; Robison, 1936; Schwartz, 1945; Short and Nye, 1958). Yet several studies have indicated that the most persistent offenders are most likely to have been referred to court (Erickson and Empey, 1963; Gold, 1966; Short and Nye, 1958). If there are changes in attitudes toward the law, one would expect to find changes in proportions of the population who became official criminals.

The third issue which will be considered is that of apparently shifting ages of criminal behavior. In 1932, Gault wrote that the most frequent age of conviction for larceny was 19 and that men convicted for assault were typically between the ages of 21 and 24. Sutherland and Cressey (1974) show that according to Uniform Crime Reports for 1971, the highest rates of arrest for committing larceny were among 15 to 17 year olds; the highest arrest rates for assault were among 18 to 20 year olds.

This comparison of patterns of criminal behavior in two generations of males were designed, in short, to provide information about whether particular types of crimes show intergenerational relationships, to determine whether attitudes of lawlessness have increased or decreased between generations, and to discover whether there have been shifts in high-risk ages for criminality.

METHOD

As part of a larger study of crime, criminal records of 506 father-son pairs had been collected through the Massachusetts Department of Corrections and the Department of Probation. Records for the fathers had been collected in 1945; records for the sons had been collected in 1975. All subjects were living in congested urban areas of eastern Massachusetts from 1936 to 1943.

To control the effects of immigration, migration, and death, pairs used for the present study met the following criteria: (1) fathers had been born in Massachusetts and were alive at age 40; (2) sons were living in Massachusetts at the age of 40 and had lived out of that state for less than 10 years. There were 115 pairs who met these criteria. Fathers had been born between 1877 and 1909. Their mean age in 1945 was 47. Sons had been born between 1926 and 1933. The mean age of the sons, in 1975, was 47. The sons had averaged 1.96 years outside of Massachusetts.

RESULTS

Father-son patterns of crime

To assess whether there are family links related to particular types of crimes, official descriptions of crimes were divided into eleven types: traffic offenses, other crimes against order (e.g., begging, vagrancy, nonsupport, bastardy), drunkenness, victimless sex crimes, white-collar business crimes, use of illegal drugs, property destruction, larceny (including auto theft, breaking and entering, and burglary), assault, rape, and murder or attempted murder. Some of these crimes (victimless sex crimes, use of illegal drugs, and property destruction) were committed by such a small number of men that statistical comparisons between generations could not be made without combining categories. Two men (both sons) were convicted for rape; for some comparisons, these crimes were grouped with assault as crimes of violence. No one in the study had been convicted for murder or attempted murder.

Among the 115 fathers, 73 had been convicted for some crime—65 for crimes other than traffic violations. Among the 115 sons, 88 had been convicted for some crime—67 for crimes other than traffic violations.

Three questions were addressed in searching for crime-specific relationships between father's and son's criminal behavior: Were there similarities between generations in terms of the first crime for which father and son had been convicted? Were there similarities between generations as measured by whether or not both father and son had committed similar types of crimes? Were there similarities between generations as measured by the most serious crime each had committed?

Among the fathers, 21 had been first convicted for a traffic offense. Their sons, however, were only slightly more likely to be first convicted for traffic violations than were sons of men who had never been convicted (38% versus 31%) or had first been convicted for a more serious crime (27%).

On the other hand, fathers whose first conviction had been for drunkenness were more likely than chance to have sons whose first conviction was for drunkenness ($p < .05$).[1] Fathers whose first conviction had been for larceny were more likely than chance to have sons whose first convictions were for larceny ($p < .01$).[2]

Six fathers were first convicted for assault. Four of their sons were first convicted for traffic violations; one had no criminal record, and one was first convicted for larceny.

Almost equal proportions of fathers (55%) and sons (64%) were first convicted for crimes less serious than their subsequent crimes. This particular "criminal style" was not more likely to occur for a son if it had occurred with his father.

Considering the entire criminal careers of fathers and sons, 92 men had been convicted for driving offenses; 98 for nontraffic crimes against order; 83 for drunkenness; 51 for larceny; and 38 for crimes of violence.

Although there was not a reliable relationship between fathers and sons committing traffic crimes, fathers who committed nontraffic crimes against order were more likely than other fathers to have sons who committed nontraffic crimes against order (p < .001; X^2 = 25.24). Also, fathers convicted for drunkenness were more likely than other fathers to have sons who had been convicted for drunkenness (p < .01; X^2 = 8.22).

Although fathers who committed larceny were not more likely than other fathers to have sons who committed larceny and fathers who committed assault were not more likely to have sons who committed assault, fathers who committed the serious crimes of larceny or assault were more likely than other fathers to have sons who committed larceny or assault (p < .05; X^2 = 4.74). Table 1 shows the intergenerational comparisons for these types of crimes.

Comparison of father's most serious crime to son's most serious crime fails to suggest crime-specific relationships on this measure.

Changes in lawlessness

To assess whether lawlessness has increased or decreased, the binomial test was used to compare the number of fathers and

Table 1: CRIMES COMMITTED BY FATHERS AND SONS

Type of Crime	Fathers	Sons	Both	Neither	(Total)
Traffic offenses	15	35	21	44	(115)
Nontraffic crimes against order	13	17	34	51	(115)
Drunkenness	22	17	22	54	(115)
Larceny	12	23	8	72	(115)
Crimes of violence	15	11	6	83	(115)
Larceny or crimes of violence	16	23	17	59	(115)

sons who committed crimes—after deleting pairs in which both father and son had been convicted. Neither crimes of violence, nor larceny, nor the combination of these crimes showed reliable differences between generations. Among all the criminal categories tested, only traffic crimes differentiated between generations: sons were much more likely than their fathers to be convicted for traffic violations ($p < .01$; $z = 2.68$).

High-risk ages

The comparison between generations reveals a striking shift in the ages when various types of crimes were first committed. Fathers had been approximately six years older than sons when first convicted for crimes against order ($p < .0001$; $t = 3.9$); approximately 10 years older when first convicted for drunkenness ($p < .0001$; $t = 6.0$); approximately 11 years older when first convicted for larceny ($p < .0001$; $t = 4.4$). Fathers, on the average, were six years older when first convicted for assault—though this difference was of borderline reliability ($p = .053$; $t = 2.0$). Table 2 shows the mean ages when fathers and sons first were convicted for these types of crimes.

In comparing fathers with their sons, a consistent pattern emerges: serious crimes were committed at younger ages by the sons. Sons were more likely than their fathers to commit crimes of violence or larceny as juveniles ($p < .0002$; $z = 3.9$). They were about as likely as their fathers to commit these types of crimes between the ages of 18 and 24. On the other hand, fathers were more likely than their sons to commit crimes of

Table 2: MEAN AGE AT FIRST CONVICTION

Type of Crime	Fathers	Sons
Crimes against order	30.0 (s.d. = 8.9)	24.4 (s.d. = 7.2)
Drunkenness	33.0 (s.d. = 8.3)	23.8 (s.d. = 5.5)
Larceny	27.8 (s.d. = 9.6)	17.1 (s.d. = 7.5)
Assault	32.2 (s.d. = 9.6)	26.2 (s.d. = 8.3)

Table 3: NUMBER OF FATHERS AND SONS CONVICTED FOR SERIOUS
CRIMES IN EACH AGE PERIOD

Age Period	Fathers	Sons	Both	Neither	(Total)
Under 18	2	22	3	88	(115)
18-24	8	12	2	93	(115)
Over 24	24	7	5	79	(115)

violence or larceny after attaining the age of 25 ($p < .005$; $z = 2.9$).

Evidence that the differences between fathers and sons cannot be attributed to increasing competence of correctional agencies or to better records in more modern periods is found in the relative rates of conviction, by age categories, for fathers and sons (see Table 3).

Whereas the proportion of fathers convicted for serious crimes increased with age, that for sons declines with age.

A somewhat different way of examining the relationship between age and generation is by looking at the age period during which each man committed his most serious crime. Excluding traffic and automobile violations (e.g., improper lights, unregistered motor vehicle), 64 fathers and 62 sons had been convicted for some crime. Among the fathers, 77% had not yet committed their most serious crime by the age of 25. Among the sons, only 31% committed a more serious crime after the age of 25 ($p < .001$).[3]

SUMMARY

Criminal records of 115 fathers and their sons, collected when each generation was approximately 47, were used to assess intergenerational patterns of crime, to evaluate whether there have been changes in the degree of lawlessness, and to learn whether the ages for high-risk criminality had altered.

The examination of patterns of crime for fathers and sons suggests that general attitudes, rather than crime-specific behaviors, are transmitted from one generation to the next. With the exception of drunkenness (and larceny as a first crime), the relationships between fathers' and sons' crimes appeared only for broad categories: nontraffic crimes against order, and combined serious crimes.

This comparison of criminal behavior for two generations gives no support to those who argue that there has been a growth in lawlessness which cannot be attributed to population changes.[4] Only for traffic crimes was there a difference in crime rates between generations; sons were more likely to have been convicted for traffic violations.

Failure to find evidence that the younger generation was more lawless than their fathers raises an interesting problem of interpretation. Few sons committed serious crimes after 1955. Of course lawlessness (as measured by proportions of populations who commit serious crimes) may have increased since that time. Alternatively, apparent increases in lawlessness may be due to increased reporting of crimes, to increased recidivism among criminals, to changes in populations, or be an artifact of a downward shift in ages during which serious crimes are being committed.

In relation to criminal behavior, the clearest difference between generations is the age at which crimes were committed. The generation reared during the 1930s, as compared with their fathers, were more likely to commit crimes in their youth and less likely to commit crimes after the age of 25.

NOTES

1. $X^2 = 4.73$, corrected for small E. Of the fathers, 23% who had been first convicted for drunkenness, as compared with 5% of other fathers, had a son whose first conviction was for drunkenness.

2. $X^2 = 6.82$, corrected for small E. Of the fathers, 50% whose first conviction was for larceny, as compared with 14% of other fathers, had a son whose first conviction was for larceny.

3. $X^2 = 26.72$. When traffic and auto crimes are included, 75% of the fathers had not yet committed their most serious crime, and 32% of the sons committed a more serious crime after the age of 25.

4. It should be noted, however, that immigrants were excluded from this study. There is some evidence that immigrants tend to be more law-abiding than native Americans (Chilton, 1946; Gault, 1932). Although there is also evidence that sons of immigrants tend to be more law-abiding than sons of native Americans (Chilton,

1946; Taft, 1936; Von Vechten, 1941), there may be an increase in lawlessness which could not be found within the scope of the present study.

REFERENCES

BELL, D. (1960). "The myth of crime waves." In The end of ideology. Glenco, Ill.: Free Press.

BLACK, D.J. (1970). "Production of crime rates." American Social Review, 35(August):733-748.

CHILTON, R.J. (1946). "Continuity in delinquency area research: A comparison of studies for Baltimore, Detroit, and Indianapolis." American Social Review, 29(February):71-83.

CHILTON, R.J. and SPIELBERGER, A. (1971). "Is delinquency increasing? Age structure and the crime rate." Social Forces, 49(March):487-493.

ERICKSON, M.L., and EMPEY, L.T. (1963). "Court records, undetected delinquency, and decision-making." Journal of Criminal Law, Criminology and Police Science, 54(December):456-469.

FARRINGTON, D.P. (1973). "Self-reports of deviant behavior: Predictive and stable?" Journal of Criminal Law and Criminology, 64(January):99-110.

FERDINAND, T.N. (1967). "The criminal patterns of Boston since 1849." American Journal of Sociology, 73(July):84-99.

——— (1970). "Demographic shifts and criminality: An inquiry." British Journal of Criminology, (April):169-175.

GAULT, R.H. (1932). Criminology. Boston: D.C. Heath.

GLUECK, S., and GLUECK, E.T. (1950). Unraveling juvenile delinquency. New York: The Commonwealth Fund.

GOLD, M. (1966). "Undetected delinquent behavior." Journal of Research in Crime and Delinquency, (January):27-46.

KITSUSE, J.I., and CICOUREL, A.V. (1963). "A note on the uses of official statistics." Social Problems, 11(fall):131-139.

LANE, R. (1976). "Criminal violence in America: The first hundred years." Annals of the American Academy of Political and Social Sciences, 423(January):1-13.

McCORD, J., McCORD, W., and HOWARD, A. (1963). "Family interaction as antecedent to the direction of male aggressiveness." Journal of Abnormal and Social Psychology, 66(3):239-242.

McCORD, W., and McCORD, J. (1959). Origins of crime. New York: Columbia University Press.

——— (1960). Origins of alcoholism. Stanford, Calif.: Stanford University Press.

MURPHEY, F.J., SHIRLEY, M.M., and WITMER, H.L. (1946). "The incidence of hidden delinquency." American Journal of Orthopsychiatry, 16(October):686-696.

PEPINSKY, H.E. (1976). "The growth of crime in the United States." Annals of the American Academy of Political and Social Science, 423(January):23-30.

PORTERFIELD, A.L. (1943). "Delinquency and its outcome in court and college." American Journal of Sociology, 44(November):199-208.

QUINNEY, R. (1971). The problem of crime. New York: Dodd, Mead.

ROBINS, L.N. (1966). Deviant children grown up. Baltimore: Williams & Wilkins.

ROBINSON, L.N. (1911). History and organization of criminal statistics in the United States. Boston: Houghton, Mifflin.

——— (1933). "History of criminal statistics (1908-1933)." Journal of Criminal Law and Criminology, 24(May-June):125-139.

ROBISON, S. (1936). Can delinquency be measured? New York: Columbia University Press.

SCHWARTZ, E.E. (1945). "A community experiment in the measurement of juvenile delinquency." National Probation Association Year Book. pp. 157-181.

SHORT, J.F. and NYE, I.F. (1958). "Extent of unrecorded juvenile delinquency: Tentative conclusions." Journal of Criminal Law, Criminology, and Police Science, 49(November-December):296-302.

SUTHERLAND, E.H. and CRESSEY, D.R. (1974). Criminology (9th ed.). Philadelphia: Lippincott.

TAFT, D.R. (1936). "Nationality and crime." American Social Review, 1(October: 724-736.

Von VECHTEN, C.C. (1941). "Criminality of the foreign-born." Journal of Criminal Law and Criminology, 32(July-August):139-147.

WILLBACH, H. (1938). "The trend of crime in New York City." Journal of Criminal Law, Criminology and Police Science, 29(May-June):62-75.

James Garofalo
*Criminal Justice Research
Center, Albany, New York*

6

TIME
A Neglected Dimension in Tests of
Criminological Theories

American criminology has proven quite fertile in the production of theories, or at least theoretical propositions. Unfortunately, little progress has been made in assessing the fidelity with which our theories represent the world around us. That is not to say that there have been no attempts to collect data and test propositions derived from the theories. On the contrary, criminological researchers have been busily applying themselves to their tasks, although generally in small-scale, unconnected, over-lapping efforts. The theme of this paper, however, is that much of the theory testing activity has suffered because it has lacked a proper amount of concern for the key dimension of time.

The deficiency is apparent in two aspects of theory testing. First, the most prominent criminological theories deal with processes of one sort or another, yet tests of these theories—or of single propositions derived from them—typically have been based on cross-sectional data. We will refer to this as a problem in the *direct testing* of theories. Second, theories are frequently investigated under the assumption that they are ahistorical, that they can be abstracted from the particular historical moments from which they derived. To keep this issue terminologically distinct, we will speak of it as a problem in *evaluating* a theory contextually. This paper concentrates on the direct testing problem. A section near the end of the paper addresses the evaluation issue briefly.

THE DIRECT TESTING OF PROCESSUAL THEORIES
WITH CROSS-SECTIONAL DATA

A paper intended primarily for criminologists, contending that the most prominent theoretical approaches in criminology emphasize process and change, seems to be arguing the obvious. At the same time, that contention is the basis of much that follows and should not be taken for granted, so some examples will be mentioned briefly.

By themselves, the key words in a number of criminological theories convey the sense of process, development, and change which the theories attempt to capture. Shaw and McKay's works (1931; 1942) are full of such terminology: "cultural transmission," "invasion," "succession," "zones of transition." Sutherland (1947:5-9) noted the importance of the time dimension by including "frequency" and "duration" as two of the sources of variability in differential association. More recently, Matza (1964) chose the word "drift" to characterize the movements of adolescents back and forth between law-abiding and delinquent behaviors. Becker (1963:24) found the idea of "career" to be "a useful conception in developing sequential models of various kinds of deviant behavior," while Wilkins (1965:91) used the concept "deviation-amplifying system" to describe the reciprocal responses and feedback between the deviant and his environment.

Although key words may not be as readily apparent in some other theories, the processual aspects are still central. Thrasher (1927) described how delinquent gangs developed from adolescent play groups. Cohen (1955) contended that the delinquent subculture was an emergent solution worked out in common by working-class boys faced with status problems. Quinney (1974) invoked the time-dependent Marxian concepts of contradiction and dialectic in his "critique of legal order" in the United States.

There is no mystery to why these prominent theories focused so closely on processes; the theorists were trying to describe life, and life *is* process. One of the reasons these theories have attained prominence is that they represent attempts to solve the problem that Nisbet (1976:94) put to the sociologist: "to obtain from such structures and types as he feels obliged to construct for analytical or conceptual purposes 'an expression of movement, of becoming, and, in short, life.' " One would expect that attempts to test aspects of these theories would be strongly sensitized to the processes and developmental sequences in the theories. Too often this has not been the case.

Some Drawbacks of Static Testing

Generally it is not possible to test all aspects of a theory in one research undertaking. Rather, propositions which predict specific results in the data are derived from the theory. Too frequently, however, the derived propositions are not ones that deal directly with the processual aspects of the theories; there seems to be a tendency to select propositions about outcomes or other static states.

One area in which this is particularly true is in the investigation of values in terms of their relevance to delinquency theories. A number of studies have used questionnaires or interviews at one point in time to determine the relationship between the degree of acceptance (or rejection) of "dominant" values and delinquent behavior (Short and Strodtbeck, 1965; Hirschi, 1969; Hindelang, 1970). Many of these studies have relied on self-reports of delinquent behavior from their adolescent subjects. Assuming that a relationship between rejection of "dominant" values and extent of delinquent behavior is uncovered in such a study, we are still left in quite a quandary. The difficulty is that human systems—individuals, groups, organizations, societies—are characterized by a high degree of what systems theorists refer to as *equifinality*. That is, the systems are capable of reaching the same end states through entirely different processes (Sutherland, 1973:23-24). Cross-sectional data do not allow us to decide among the competing hypotheses that rejection of the values led to delinquency, that involvement in delinquent behavior led to a rejection of the values as an ego-protection technique, or that the rejection and the behavior reciprocally influence each other. By the same token, finding no association between values and delinquent behavior in cross-sectional data does not invalidate the possibility of a time-dependent episodic relationship between the two, similar to what is described by Matza. If the subjects tested are randomly distributed across different stages of "drift," a real relationship between values and delinquency could be effectively masked, or at least attenuated.[1]

There are some cases where static analysis of predicted states or outcomes could prove useful rather than misleading as partial tests of criminological theories—i.e., the outpouring of cross-sectional studies dealing with the distribution of delinquency in the class structure (Nye, et al., 1958; Akers, 1964; Empey and Erickson, 1966; Voss, 1966; Williams and Gold, 1972). But the most interesting aspects of theories are their descriptions of processes and change, not their predictions about static states. An understanding of the processes certainly allows us to make more accurate predictions, but being able to predict static states does not necessarily mean that we have grasped the processes leading to those states. It is in testing how well a theory adds to our *understanding* that a sensitivity to the dimension of time is required.

There has been a great deal written about techniques of causal analysis that can be used with cross-sectional data (Blalock, 1964, 1971; Hirschi and Selvin, 1973; Duncan, 1975). Ultimately, however, techniques such as path analysis cannot definitely determine the time ordering of variables. In fact, there are great dangers in being misled by the dynamic terminology surrounding essentially static statistical procedures. Words such as "covariation," "effects," and "controlling for" can easily lull one into making unspoken analogies with true experimental designs in which actual changes are introduced in the units of analysis. Great caution must be taken in trying to infer the nature of changes in the real world from the pencil and paper manipulations of statistical techniques. For example, the slope of a regression line is often said to indicate the amount of *change* in a dependent variable associated with a unit *change* in an independent variable. But in the case where the extent of individual involvement in criminal behavior is regressed on social class position (and assuming a negative relationship exists), it would be grossly misleading to conclude that criminal behavior would decrease by a certain amount if a certain number of individuals actually changed their class position upward. The data show only how criminal behavior is distributed in a particular class structure at one point in time; they say nothing about the possible effects of a change in the class structure. Similarly, cross-sectional correlation analysis of the relationship between homicide and the death penalty or delinquency and unemployment cannot reveal what would happen to homicide rates if States began to inflict the death penalty frequently or to delinquency rates if unemployment were to drop by some given percent.

Another way that research on processes using cross-sectional data can be misleading is by creating the "illusion of movement" (Nisbet, 1976:96). Such an illusion is produced by *inferring* the existence of a particular process from data collected on different subjects or objects *assumed* to be located at various points within the process. A good example is provided in a recent book on cross-cultural perceptions of deviance (Newman, 1976). The author, using cross-sectional data, finds that there is more variation in perceptions of deviance in more industrialized ("developed") nations than in less developed nations. The inference is then made that this indicates some evolutionary movement: as societies become more complex and differentiated, perceptions of deviance become more differentiated. Yet, no changes were actually observed during the course of the study. Regardless of whether the author's inference is true or not, his data only project an "illusion of movement," not real evolutionary change.

The "illusion of movement" is also created by the implicit conceptualization of some variables in cross-sectional research. This is apparent in the way age is often used. Information from a cross-sectional sample containing subjects of different ages is used to make statements about how a behavior (e.g., criminality) is related to the *aging process*. In fact, such data reveal nothing of the sort; they only describe how the behavior is distributed in the age structure at *one point in time*. The researcher making statements about the aging process from such data is assuming that the earlier behavior of the older subjects in the study is adequately represented by the behavior of the younger subjects in the study. This assumption should at least be made explicit.[2]

An example that essentially parallels the conceptual problems with age is Wheeler's (1961) test of Clemmer's "prisonization" hypothesis. Wheeler used interviews with a cross-section of inmates to test changes in conformity to staff expectations over time by classifying the inmates according to the length of time they had served (or whether they were in the early, middle, or late stage of their incarceration). Then, just as is often done with cross-sectional data on age, Wheeler inferred *changes* from the *differences* that existed at one point in time.

Special Problems with Recall Data

The most common substitute for actual measurement or observation across time in criminological theory testing is the use of data gathered from subjects who are asked to recall events that occurred at some time in the past. Becker (1963), for example, used recall interviews to test his theoretical notions about the sequential development of marijuana use. For this type of testing the researcher must depend on the ability of the subject, *first*, to remember whether or not certain events

Table 1: "WERE YOU EVER PICKED UP, OR CHARGED BY THE POLICE, FOR ANY (OTHER)* REASON WHETHER OR NOT YOU WERE GUILTY?"

| | Age of Respondent | | | | |
	25 or younger	26-35	36-50	50 or older	Total**
Yes	20% (46)	13% (38)	11% (42)	6% (30)	11% (156)
No	80% (188)	87% (251)	89% (340)	94% (497)	89% (1,296)

*Other than for a traffic violation.

**Thirteen respondents of races other than white or black and one respondent who replied "don't know" are excluded.

Source: 1973 General Social Survey. See National Data Program for the Social Sciences, 1973.

occured and, *second*, to accurately place those events in time.

In trying to determine how well subjects remember whether an event occurred at all, consider Table 1. Note that the question on which the table is based is open-ended with respect to time; it asks, "Were you *ever*...?" Yet the youngest age group—in which respondents have a maximum time reference of 25 years—shows a rate of police contact that is more than three times greater than the rate for respondents in the oldest age group who are using a minimum time reference of 50 years. These data, from a national survey, are amenable to several different interpretations. They support the proposition that U.S. society, during the past 50 years, has become increasingly dependent on formal means of social control. Thus, assuming that young people (e.g., 16-25) have continued to be high probability targets for law enforcement throughout the 50-year period, older survey respondents would have spent the high-risk-of-arrest age in an historical period when formal rule enforcement was not as strongly emphasized. However, the data are equally consistent with the methodological artifact of forgetting coupled with the substantive proposition of no significant changes in formal rule enforcement practices over the past 50 years. Again assuming that the high-risk-of-arrest age has been 16-25 during the past 50 years, police contacts would have occurred more recently for younger respondents and, therefore, would be remembered more often.

Even if respondents can accurately recall the occurrence or nonoccurrence of certain events, the testing of processual theories imposes an additional requirement—namely, that the recalled events be correctly *ordered* in time. Of course, the further back in time subjects are asked to recall, the more acute the problem of correctly ordering events becomes. The size of this problem can be illustrated with the results of a methodological test of victimization survey techniques in which samples of the population are interviewed to determine the extent and nature of victimizations that respondents may have suffered during some specified period preceding the interviews.

In January 1971 a victimization survey was conducted by the U.S. Bureau of the Census in Santa Clara County (San Jose),

California. Included with the sample from the general population were 620 persons whose names appeared in the San Jose police department files as having been victims of certain types of crime during the preceding 12 months (known victims). Interviewers were not aware that some of the names had been sampled from police files. Later, the responses from known victims who had been interviewed were examined to determine how well they remembered the correct month in which the incident occurred, using the date of occurrence from the police report as the criterion. Table 2 shows the proportion of incidents correctly placed in time (i.e., correct month) by how many months prior to the interview the incidents occurred. The rather low and rapidly declining percentages indicate either that the criterion for determining when the incident occurred (the police report) was faulty[3] or that respondents had trouble remembering what might be considered fairly noteworthy events (robbery, assault, rape, burglary, and larceny). Remem-

Table 2: CASES SAMPLED FROM SAN JOSE POLICE FILES BY TIME PERIOD IN WHICH INCIDENT OCCURRED BY WHETHER REPORTED IN SURVEY INTERVIEW AS OCCURRING DURING SAME TIME PERIOD.

Appearing in police records as having occurred:	Number of cases	Percentage reporting correct time period to interviewer
1 month ago	36	67%
2	34	56
3	31	55
4	32	38
5	32	28
6	36	39
7	36	36
8	33	33
9	34	32
10	29	34
11	27	11
12 months ago	34	38
Total*	394	40%

*Of the original 620 cases sampled, 226 were not interviewed, most (195) because they could not be located or had moved from the area.

Source: Adapted from Table G in U.S. Department of Justice (1972).

ber also that the question in Table 2 is whether the incident was placed in the proper *month*. There may be times that an adequate test of a theory requires even more precise placement of events in time.

The substantial decrease in recall ability for more and more distant events is especially problematic in criminological research. Researchers in this discipline are often attempting to study events that do not occur with relatively great frequency or regularity, e.g., very serious criminal behavior. When using techniques such as victimization or self-report delinquency surveys, the problem of uncovering a sufficient number of events for analytic purposes can be solved in two ways: question a very large sample of respondents about recent events, or question a smaller sample about events that may have occurred during a time frame that extends further into the past (use a longer reference period).[4] The latter option is usually employed because, in contrast to increasing sample size, it does not create additional costs. Thus we have delinquency researchers asking respondents about events that may have occurred during reference periods ranging from one (Clark and Wenninger, 1962; Hindelang, 1973) to three (Gold, 1970; Williams and Gold, 1972) years ago, or at any time at all during the past (Voss, 1966; West, 1973).[5]

Given the results (Table 2) of the San Jose methodological test in which a one-year reference period was used, analyses of recall data that involve time ordering issues must be viewed with a bit of skepticism. Such is the case with Gold's (1970) attempt to gauge the effect of apprehension by the police on subsequent delinquent behavior. The method used involves matching respondents within age/sex groups. One member of the pair reported (recalled) being apprehended by the police while the other revealed no apprehension. Pairs were formed so that each member had approximately equal numbers of recalled delinquencies prior to the time when the one member was apprehended. The number of delinquencies for each member recalled as occurring after that time were then compared. Gold's results, for that aspect of his analysis, rely on how well his adolescent respondents were able to place their delinquent involvements in time over a three-year reference period. His data (1970:138-139) indicate that memory effects, causing the misplacement of a few events in time by each respondent, might have altered the results considerably.[6]

In addition to the problem of simply forgetting, methods that rely on recall also have to deal with the possibility of subjects reinterpreting events in their own biographies as they try to give coherent accounts of some aspect of their lives. This issue may not be as salient when asking a number of subjects to recall specific types of events, but it comes to the fore when trying to reconstruct, in detail, the variety of processes and changes that have influenced the behaviors of one or a small number of subjects over a long span of time—the type of data that goes directly to the core of, for example, labeling theory or differential association. Life history studies in the tradition of Shaw (1930) and Sutherland (1937) are especially prone to the reinterpretation problem, as are more recent works which attempt to reconstruct processes through in-depth recall interviews with a limited number of subjects (e.g., Letkemann, 1973; Jackson, 1974).

An appreciation of the reinterpretation problem in recall methods is attainable from the phenomenological perspective. Subjects in recall interviews are trying to communicate their past experience to the interviewer in a meaningful way; they are not simply spewing forth data which has been recorded at some prior time, stored, and left unmodified by ensuing experiences. In order to be successfully communicated, the subject's history must have some coherence. The portrait of a subject's life between the ages of 10 and 25 might differ radically depending on whether the interview is conducted when the subject is 30 or 50 years old; 20 years of additional experiences can easily modify the meaning attributed to past experience.

The interviewer is implicated in the problem also. If we follow the suggestion of the phenomenologists to use an "interpretive paradigm," in which "all social reality is seen as the outcome of ongoing negotiation processes" (Dreitzel, 1970: xiii), then we must view the recall interview as the social construction of a record of the respondent's past experiences accomplished through interviewer/subject negotiation. From this perspective, the interviewer is not perceived as a passive recorder of the subject's experiences. Both persons are seen as actively involved in producing an account of the experiences.

Some Exceptions to the Rule

The preceding discussion of the many difficulties involved in trying to test criminological theories adequately with cross-sectional data should not leave the impression that longitudinal or time series data have never been used in criminology. On the contrary, some of the more notable contributions to criminological research have been longitudinal in approach: Shaw and McKay's (1931, 1942) ecological work, the follow-up studies conducted by the Gluecks (e.g., 1950, 1968), the self-concept investigations of Dinitz et al. (1962), Miller's (1966, 1967) observations of delinquent gangs, the Elliot and Voss (1974) study of delinquency and school dropout, the Philadelphia cohort study (Wolfgang et al., 1972), some historical investigations (e.g., Gusfield, 1963; Platt, 1969; Rothman, 1971), and so on. The problem is that, relative to the total volume of research, such studies are a minority.

The Shaw and McKay and the Elliot and Voss works are particularly enlightening on the subject of the need for longitudinal data. In both cases, major conclusions would have been different if the researchers had used cross-sectional data. Shaw and McKay, for example, had official Chicago delinquency data for the same urban areas across a number of years. They noted that the data showed relationships between the proportions of certain ethnic and racial groups in city areas and the delinquency rates for the areas. But because their data extended across time, they were able to carry the analysis further:

> One might be led to assume that the relatively large number of boys brought into court is due to the presence of certain racial or national groups were it not for the fact that the population composition of many of these neighborhoods has changed completely, without appreciable change in their rank as to rates of delinquents. [Shaw and McKay, 1942:155].

Thus, their data tended to support the urban ecological theory of the Chicago school and to emphasize the importance of physical environment.

Elliot and Voss note early in their book that the "most important limitation of existing research on delinquency and dropout is the almost exclusive reliance on cross-sectional designs" (1974:7). Their study was based on longitudinal data, and their results with respect to delinquent behavior and dropout are telling testimony of the necessity to look at events over time. Although they found that adolescents in their sample who eventually dropped out of school committed more delinquent acts, during the full time frame of the study, than subjects who eventually graduated, the patterns of delinquency across time were quite different for dropouts and graduates. The dropouts showed an increasing trend in delinquency through their school years, but their delinquency decreased dramatically after dropping out. In fact, after dropout they showed less involvement with delinquency than the subjects who remained in school. The finding supported Elliot and Voss' predictions about the dynamic processes implicated in both delinquency and dropout.

Mention of these two studies is not meant to imply that they represent the ideal for criminological research; both have aspects that can be criticized. But they do illustrate how cross-sectional data can be misleading if it is used to test theories about process and change.

Reasons for the Lack of Longitudinal Research

When a researcher is reporting cross-sectional results and recognizes that the data do not adequately test the theoretical propositions under consideration and that longitudinal data are needed, the problem is generally handled by pointing out that "ideal data are not available" or that "further research is needed." Behind these phrases exist some very stern realities that influence the relative rarity of longitudinal research.

First, the nature of research funding does not encourage long-term projects. The life spans of supportive grants are generally one or two years; even a duration of four years is unusual. The reasons for the particular nature of research funding in the

United States deserve investigation, but that topic is beyond the scope of this paper.

Second, most of the research oriented toward the testing of criminological theories is performed by persons in academic institutions, and they are under a great deal of pressure to produce findings quickly. The "publish or perish" imperative within academic career structures is not conducive to long-term research projects, especially for people who are in the early stages of their careers. Even for tenured professors, wider recognition in the discipline is strongly connected to continuing, frequent publication.

Third, the training of most criminologists is heavily influenced by sociology, a discipline in which research into change and process has not been emphasized in recent years.[7] The cross-sectional survey has become the dominant methodology, and statistical manipulations are often accepted as substitutes for the measurement of actual change—a problem that was discussed earlier. In fact, criminologists trained in sociology generally must turn to either the psychological testing or econometric literature for guidance in how to measure change.

Finally, there has been a suggestion that very long-term research projects would still be at a premium even if the problems of funding, career pressures, and training could be overcome. Referring to a study that might last as long as 30 years, Hyman (1972:15) observed:

> The initial population under study would have aged, but so too would the investigator! One must have a healthy-minded attitude, and contemplate the future with great self-confidence if one is to undertake a study that is as long as the average professional lifetime of most scholars. To begin something that one may not live to see the end of requires a capacity for transcending the self and finding gratification simply in the thought that one is laying down the baselines others will exploit. . . . The record suggest that there are few among us who are driven in this way.

Thus, Hyman claims that there is a psychological resistance to longitudinal research, at least when the time frame involved is very long.

The question to be addressed briefly in the next section is: How can we face these realities that impede longitudinal research and still improve theory testing by taking the dimension of time into consideration?

INCORPORATING TIME
INTO DIRECT TESTS OF THEORIES

Ideally, all theoretical propositions could be tested with multiple observations of the same subjects over a long period of time with an experimental procedure involving control groups and the ability of the researcher to manipulate some of the variables. Fortunately, there are several techniques which depart from the ideal, yet which allow us to approximate more rigorous tests of change and process, at least with regard to some theoretical issues. Space constraints do not permit extensive descriptions of such techniques, but some will be mentioned here to illustrate the possibilities.

Historical Research

Earlier in the paper some exceptions to the reliance on cross-sectional analysis were mentioned, and among them were several historical studies (Gusfield, 1963; Platt, 1969; Rothman, 1971). Of course, the term "historical research" can apply to any investigation of events that occurred in the past, in which case such diverse undertakings as victimization surveys, the birth cohort study of Wolfgang et al. (1972), and Gusfield's (1963) analysis of the prohibition movement would be included. However, the term is restricted here to the ex post facto investigation of records and observations that were made contemporaneously with the events (thus, excluding recall surveys). Furthermore, it is recognized that some historical research endeavors are more "historical" than others; the Philadelphia birth cohort researchers could have collected the school and police data they used as it became available (probably without affecting their results), but it would not have been very practical for Gusfied to gather his data firsthand.

The ability to conduct historical research depends, to a great extent, on the availability of records, and this frequently leads to a reliance on official records because they are usually the most systematic available. By now, all researchers should be well aware of the many problems with official records (Kitsuse and Cicourel, 1963; Douglas, 1971). However, there are cases when official data might be *superior* to other sources of information in historical research. Nash (1970), for example, contends that a more valid account of the character and changes of colonial American social structure can be obtained through analysis of such sources as tax lists and probate documents than through reliance on the diaries, correspondence, and other written material left by the most literate and visible members of colonial society.

The past provides a wealth of events that can be used to test theoretical propositions in criminology. This is especially true for propositions from theories that address themselves to more encompassing levels of social organization (e.g., ecological or Marxian conflict theories). The growing use of historical materials in criminology is encouraging, particularly in light of the comments on the ahistorical character of much theory testing that will be made later.

Secondary Analysis of Data from Previous Research

Making a distinction between secondary analysis and historical research is really arbitrary. The reason for the distinction is to highlight the advantages of using data that were systematically collected in previous studies. First, the researcher often has information that allows a reasonable assessment of the quality of such data—e.g., descriptions of the sampling and the data collection techniques used, copies of the exact questions asked, and so on. Second, the existence of data libraries and the fact that comparable information has been gathered on some topics over a number of years help to ensure that relevant data are easily accessible.

Secondary analysis of a series of studies generally does not provide information about the *same individuals* over time. Thus, we can rarely reproduce a panel design with secondary analysis, but we can look at trends. For example, to avoid the previously mentioned problem of making inferences about the aging process from cross-sectional data, we might use information from a series of comparable studies as a quasi-panel (Hyman, 1972:275). That is, the responses of 20-year-old subjects in a 1950 survey are compared to the responses of 30-year-olds in a 1960 survey and to 40-year-old subjects in a 1970 survey.

It is true that political scientists and sociologists (in specialities other than deviance) will find the stringing together of results from previous surveys to examine trends much more fruitful than will criminologists, mainly because of the topics (e.g., political preferences, attitudes toward work) that have been repeated most often in surveys. But the whole area of using secondary analysis to examine change and process over time has been left virtually unexplored by criminologists.[8] With ample caution (cf., Hyman, 1972), it probably can prove quite useful.

Natural Quasi-experiments

A potentially valuable approach for researchers interested in testing propositions about change and process is to take advantage of situations where changes are introduced in the natural world by persons or agencies other than the researcher. There are a number of design variations that are applicable to quasi-experimentation and that have been described extensively in terms of technique, strengths, and weaknesses (Campbell and Stanley, 1963; Caporaso and Roos, 1973).

In criminology, natural quasi-experiments have been found most frequently in evaluation studies of correctional measures.[9] But correctional measures are regularly imposed. We are more interested here in changes that are more unique—e.g., a legal or economic change. Chambliss (1966) and Campbell and Ross (1968), for example, have utilized natural quasi-experimental situations involving changes in official enforcement policies (for parking and speeding violations, respectively), and their results provide tests for some of the propositions in deterrence theory.

Often it is necessary to rely on official data or secondary analysis of previous research to obtain prechange (or even postchange) information in quasi-experiments. On other occasions, researchers may be able to anticipate interesting changes and perform their own data collection in stages, so that what might have been a simple cross-sectional study initially is transformed into a quasi-experimental study. In either case, to capitalize on natural quasi-experimental situations requires a bit of imagination, or at least an openness to what is happening in the world.

Simulations[10]

Because it is not always economical or even possible to observe the processes postulated by some theory, it may be helpful to simulate the processes. For example, Shoham and his colleagues (1973) were interested in testing some propositions about the patterns of face-to-face interaction that result in violence. Such patterns have been investigated with recall interviews (Toch, 1969), but, obviously, it is difficult to systematically observe such patterns as they naturally occur. One of the research techniques used by Shoham was role playing to simulate interactions leading to violence; subjects acted out situations that were expected to have high potentials for violent outcomes. Simulations have been used with greater frequency in studies of more formal decision-making processes, such as parole and sentencing decisions (Wilkins et al., 1973; Zimmerman, 1976).

Perhaps the main argument against using simulations to test theoretical processes is that simulations are based on representations (models) of human systems and, by definition, cannot be perfect replications of the "real world." Doubt is cast on whether the results of simulations can be reliably generalized to the world outside the simulated situation. However, we must recognize that different models of the same system vary in the degree to which they adequately represent the system and that this variation ranges along a continuum from absolute lack of identity to absolute identity (in which case the "model" ceases to be a model). As with taking advantage of quasi-experimental situations, the success of simulations depends heavily on the imagination and creativity of the researcher—in this instance, on the researcher's ability to approximate "real world" conditions as closely as possible.

TIME AND THE CONTEXTUAL EVALUATION OF THEORIES

All of the preceding sections of this paper have dealt with the issue of time as it pertains to what has been called the direct testing of theories. Time has been treated as a dimension that exists in the processes and changes postulated by many criminological theories, and the necessity for researchers to take that dimension into account has been stressed. As noted at the outset of the paper, theories must also be evaluated in terms of the particular historical moments from which they derive. From this perspective, time is viewed as a dimension that is both internal and external to a theory. There are two conceptually distinct, but related, questions involved here: (a) How adequately does the theory incorporate a "sense of history," an understanding of the historical developments leading to the phenomena it describes (time internal)? (b) To what extent are the particulars of the theory dependent on the historical, biographical, and structural situation of the theorist (time external)?

The first question basically expands the scope of what has been discussed so far. Most prominent criminological theories do postulate certain processes and changes, and time-sensitive methods must be used to test them, but the extent to which those processes and changes are unique to a specific historical moment within a specific social structure must also be evaluated. In other words, we should be wary of accepting those processes and changes as ahistorical generalizations, even when they have survived direct testing. This is generally what Phillipson had in mind when he questioned the utility of generalizing some American delinquency theories to the English situation, given the differences in history and structure that exist (1974:163-170). If that transfer is problematic, how much more so are attempts to generalize to earlier periods in history or to countries such as China? The "sense of history" issue is not new by any means; Mills (1959; Ch. 8), for example, expressed a great deal of concern about it in relation to sociology. Still, the issue has been neglected by criminological researchers in favor of the direct testing of theoretical propositions.

As noted, the second question (time external to the theory)

can be treated as conceptually distinct from the first, but they are certainly not independent. The historical/structural location of the theorist (time external to the theory) can strongly affect the particular "sense of history," if any, expressed in the theory (time internal to the theory). The conceptual distinction is made here solely for heuristic purposes.

When Mills contended that the proper areas for study by the social sciences were to be found at the "co-ordinate points" of biography, history, and society (1959:143), he must have been aware—judging from his earlier work (Mills, 1943)—that the same schema could be turned inward and applied to the social sciences themselves. That is, the locations of *theorists* along the three coordinates can be useful data in trying to evaluate theories. Essentially, this is a problem in the sociology of knowledge, and solutions have been proposed that range all the way from crude materialism (ideas are merely reflections of existing socioeconomic structures) to crude idealism (ideas are autonomous of socioeconomic structures). However, the problem should at least be addressed from some perspective by criminologists.

One possible approach is to take a Marxian perspective on the problem. Marx's writings contain a number of observations on a dialectical interpretation of the history of ideas—what Swingewood calls a "theory of theory" in which "Marx does not reduce social theory simply to the level of reflecting economic interests, but postulates... the *dialectical* development of social thought, the contradictory, uneven relation between the social theorist, his group and class, society and history" (1975:71). The Marxian perspective allows an evaluation of theories within their historical context because, according to Swingewood, it is based on the idea of an intimate connection between the content of theory and the *praxis* of the theorist, because it deals with knowledge and society in a dialectical rather than unidirectional fashion, and because it recognizes the important mediating effect of the changing position of the theorist's class (i.e., dominant, rising, declining).

The last point cited—the mediating effect of class—is particularly important because it tends to deal with both of the questions posed in this section. The theorist is located in a class at a particular moment (time external), and the position of that class within society has an effect on how the theorist places his or her ideas within the context of history (time internal). Swingewood (1975:65-68) provides an example of how Marx applied that perspective to an evaluation of the economic theories of Adam Smith, Ricardo, and Malthus.

There is no intention here to argue that the Marxian perspective is the correct one from which to evaluate theories contextually. However, given the fact that only a few works have investigated this problem in criminology (e.g., Snodgrass, 1972; Boostrom, 1974), a consideration of that perspective at least provides a focal point for raising the relevant questions.

SUMMARY

We have considered the dimension of time, as it pertains to criminological theories, from a number of different angles. Most attention has been given to the direct testing of processes and changes postulated in the theories. The discussion of that issue involved a critique of the common practice of using static, cross-sectional data to test theoretical notions about change and process, a discussion of why the practice predominates, and a brief overview of some techniques that can be used to take time into account as a dimension in theories.

In the final section of the paper, time was treated as a dimension to be considered so that criminological theories could be evaluated within their historical context. This involved two overlapping issues: the "sense of history" expressed by the theory, and the effects of the historical/structural location of the theorist.

In testing and evaluating theories, researchers should use methods that do justice to the content of the theories and that allow a full exploration of the implications of the theories. If the dimension of time in its several senses is neglected, those tasks can be only partially accomplished.

NOTES

1. Finding a relationship, however, would tend to falsify a theory that predicted no relationship.

2. As a corollary, researchers using data on the same subjects across time should be wary of treating a possibly dynamic variable as static. That is, the scores of individuals on some variables measured early in the study (e.g., socioeconomic status, family situation) should be reassessed at later times rather than assumed to stay constant throughout the study.

3. However, this would not explain the decreasing percentages across the recall period.

4. Actually, there is another technique used often; trivial (or at least less serious) violations are investigated because they occur with relatively great frequency.

5. For an investigation of the effects of using an open-ended reference period to measure self-reported delinquency, see Smith and Cartwright (1965).

6. This does not mean that Gold's results are erroneous; they may accurately reflect, or even understate, the effects of apprehension. The example is given only to illustrate the problematic nature of the evidence pertaining to our theoretical propositions about change and process. For a criticism of Gold's matching procedure on other grounds, see Hirschi (1975:200-201).

7. Of course, there are a number of criminologists with academic backgrounds in psychology, and their training, in many cases, has prepared them to test theories of change and process because of an emphasis on experimental design. Also, in sociology, there appears to be a growing realization of the need for data gathered through observation, participant observation, and other time-oriented techniques, but the extent to which this realization has penetrated research methods and statistics courses is questionable.

8. Curtis (1974:24-31) did depend on some secondary analysis of other studies to test theoretical notions about trends in interracial crime.

9. Actually, many of the evaluation studies use what Campbell and Stanley (1963:8) refer to as "pre-experimental" rather than quasi-experimental designs.

10. Although not treated separately here, gaming techniques are viewed as a subset of simulation methods by the author.

REFERENCES

AKERS, R. (1964). "Socioeconomic status and delinquent behavior: A retest." Journal of Research in Crime and Delinquency, 1:38-46.

BECKER, H.S. (1963). Outsiders. New York: Free Press.

BLALOCK, H.M., Jr. (1964). Causal inferences in nonexperimental research. Chapel Hill: University of North Carolina Press.

––– (1971). Causal models in the social sciences. Chicago: Aldine.

BOOSTROM, R.L. (1974). "The personalization of evil: The emergence of American criminology, 1865-1910." Ph.D. dissertation. University of California, Berkeley.

CAMPBELL, D.T., and STANLEY, J.C. (1963). Experimental and quasi-experimental designs for research. Chicago: Rand McNally.

CAMPBELL, D.T., and ROSS, H.L. (1968). "The Connecticut crackdown on speeding." Law and Society Review, 3:33-53.

CAPORASO, J.A., and ROOS, L.L., Jr. (eds., 1973). Quasi-experimental approaches. Evanston, Ill.: Northwestern University Press.

CHAMBLISS, W.J. (1966). "The deterrent influence of punishment." Crime and Delinquency, 12:70-75.

CLARK, J., and WENNINGER, E. (1962). "Socio-economic class and areas as correlates of illegal behavior among juveniles." American Sociological Review, 27:826-834.

COHEN, A.K. (1955). Delinquent boys. New York: Free Press.

CURTIS, L.A. (1974). Criminal violence. Lexington, Mass.: Lexington Books.

DINITZ, S., SCARPITTI, F.R., and RECKLESS, W.C. (1962). "Delinquency vulnerability: A cross group and longitudinal analysis." American Social Review, 28:515-517.

DOUGLAS, J.D. (1971). American social order. New York: Free Press.

DREITZEL, H.P. (ed., 1970). Recent sociology, no. 2. New York: Macmillan.

DUNCAN, O.D. (1975). Introduction to structural equation models. New York: Academic Press.

ELLIOT, D.S., and VOSS, H.L. (1974). Delinquency and dropout. Lexington, Mass.: Lexington Books.

EMPEY, L., and ERICKSON, M. (1966). "Hidden delinquency and social status." Social Forces, 44:546-554.

GLUECK, S., and GLUECK, E. (1950). Unraveling juvenile delinquency. New York: Commonwealth Fund.

——— (1968). Delinquents and nondelinquents in perspective. Cambridge, Mass.: Harvard University Press.

GOLD, M. (1970). Delinquent behavior in an American city. Belmont, Calif.: Brooks/Cole.

GUSFIELD, J.R. (1963). Symbolic crusade. Urbana, Ill.: University of Illinois Press.

HINDELANG, M.J. (1970). "The commitment of delinquents to their misdeeds: Do delinquents drift?" Social Problems, 17:502-509.

——— (1973). "Causes of delinquency: A partial replication and extension." Social Problems, 20:471-487.

HIRSCHI, T. (1969). Causes of delinquency. Berkeley: University of California Press.

——— (1975). "Labelling theory and juvenile delinquency: An assessment of the evidence." Pp. 181-203 in W.R. Gove (ed.), The labelling of deviance. New York: Halsted Press (a Sage publication).

HIRSCHI, T., and SELVIN, H.C. (1973). Principles of survey analysis. New York: Free Press.

HYMAN, H.H. (1972). Secondary analysis of sample surveys. New York: John Wiley.

JACKSON, B. (1974). In the life. New York: New American Library.

KITSUSE, J.I., and CICOUREL, A.V. (1963). "A note on the uses of official statistics." Social Problems, 11:131-139.

LETKEMANN, P. (1973). Crime as work. Englewood Cliffs, N.J.: Prentice-Hall.

MATZA, D. (1964). Delinquency and drift. New York: John Wiley.

MILLER, W.B. (1966). "Violent crimes in city gangs." Annals, 364:97-112.

——— (1967). "Theft behavior in city gangs." Pp. 25-37 in M.W. Klein (ed.), Juvenile gangs in context. Englewood Cliffs, N.J.: Prentice-Hall.

MILLS, C.W. (1943). "The professional ideology of social pathologists." American Journal of Sociology, 49:165-80.

——— (1959). The sociological imagination. New York: Oxford University Press.

NASH, G.B. (1970). Class and society in early America. Englewood Cliffs, N.J.: Prentice-Hall.

National Data Program for the Social Sciences (1973). Codebook for the Spring 1973 General Social Survey. Williamstown, Mass.: Roper Public Opinion Research Center.

NEWMAN, G. (1976). Comparative deviance. New York: Elsevier.

NISBET, R. (1976). Sociology as an art form. New York: Oxford University Press.

NYE, F.I., SHORT, J., Jr., and OLSON, V. (1958). "Socioeconomic status and delinquent behavior." American Journal of Sociology, 63:381-389.

PHILLIPSON, M. (1974). Understanding crime and delinquency. Chicago: Aldine.

PLATT, A.M. (1969). The child savers. Chicago: University of Chicago Press.

QUINNEY, R. (1974). Critique of legal order. Boston: Little, Brown.

ROTHMAN, D.J. (1971). The discovery of the asylum. Boston: Little, Brown.

SHAW, C.R. (1930). The jack-roller. Chicago: University of Chicago Press.

SHAW, C.R., and McKAY, H.D. (1931). Social factors in juvenile delinquency. Volume II of report on the causes of crime. National Commission on Law Observance and Enforcement. Washington, D.C.: U.S. Government Printing Office.

SHAW, C.R., and McKAY, H.D. (1942). Juvenile delinquency and urban areas. Chicago: University of Chicago Press.

SHOHAM, S., BEN-DAVID, S., VADMANI, R., ATAR, J., and FLEMIN, S. (1973). "The cycles of interaction in violence." In S. Shoham, R. Marcuse, and S. Fleming (eds.), Israeli Studies in Criminology (Vol. II). Jerusalem: Jerusalem Academic Press.

SHORT, J.F., Jr., and STRODTBECK, F.L. (1965). Group process and gang delinquency. Chicago: University of Chicago Press.

SMITH, D.O., and CARTWRIGHT, D.S. (1965). "Two measures of reported delinquent behavior." American Sociological Review 30:573-576.

SNODGRASS, J. (1972). "The American criminological tradition: Portraits of the men and ideology in a discipline." Ph.D. dissertation. University of Pennsylvania, Philadelphia.

SUTHERLAND, E.H. (1937). The professional thief. Chicago: University of Chicago Press.

——— (1947). Principles of criminology (4th ed.). Philadelphia: Lippincott.

SUTHERLAND, J.W. (1973). A general systems philosophy for the social and behavioral sciences. New York: George Braziller.

SWINGEWOOD, A. (1975). Marx and modern social theory. London: Macmillan.

THRASHER, F.M. (1927). The gang. Chicago: University of Chicago Press.

TOCH, H. (1969). Violent men. Chicago: Aldine.

U.S. Department of Justice (1972). San Jose Methods Test of Known Crime Victims. Law Enforcement Assistance Administration, Satistics Division. Washington, D.C.: U.S. Government Printing Office.

VOSS, H. (1966). "Socio-economic status and reported delinquent behavior." Social Problems, 13:314-324.

WEST, D.J. (1973). Who becomes delinquent? London: Heinemann.

WHEELER, S. (1961). "Socialization in correctional communities." American Sociological Review, 26:697-712.

WILKINS, L.T. (1965). Social deviance. Englewood Cliffs, N.J.: Prentice-Hall.

WILKINS, L.T., GOTTFREDSON, D.M., ROBISON, J.O., and SADOWSKY, C.A.

(1973). Information selection and use in parole decision-making. Parole Decision-Making Project, Supplemental Report no. 5. Davis, Calif.: National Council on Crime and Delinquency.

WILLIAMS, J., and GOLD, M. (1972). "From delinquent behavior to official delinquency." Social Problems, 20:209-229.

WOLFGANG, M.E., FIGLIO, R.M., and SELLIN, T. (1972). Delinquency in a birth cohort. Chicago: University of Chicago Press.

ZIMMERMAN, S. (1976). "Sentencing councils: A study by simulation." Ph.D. dissertation. State University of New York, Albany.

W. William Minor
University of Maryland

7

A DETERRENCE-CONTROL
THEORY OF CRIME

Although general deterrence is a major element in the rationale
of formal legal sanctioning (see Walker, 1971, for others), the
concept suffers from both imprecise theoretical conceptualization and inadequate empirical examination. The purpose of
the research reported herein, therefore, is twofold: First, to
integrate the deterrence paradigm with a more complete theory
of social conformity and deviance; second, to subject the result-
ant theoretical formulation to empirical examination through
appropriate research methods, in this case, a community survey
of perceptions, attitudes, and behaviors.

Briefly, we may identify three major problems in deterrence
theory and research: *Causal order, contingency,* and *theoretical
integration.*

The problem of causal order confounds the two major
approaches to research on deterrence, official-data studies, and
perception/self-report studies. Briefly, the official-data studies
(e.g., Gibbs, 1968; Tittle, 1969; Tittle and Rowe, 1974) relate
crime rates to characteristics of sanctions across different political units. Because crime rates influence sanctions (Schwartz,

AUTHOR'S NOTE: The author wishes to express his appreciation to Charles
Wellford, Ray Tennyson, Theodore Chiricos, and Gordon Waldo for their helpful
suggestions, and to the computing centers of Florida State University and the
University of Maryland for computer support.

1968; Campbell and Ross, 1968; Bowers and Salem, 1972; Bowers, 1974), however, as well as the other way around, the interpretation of such associations between crime rates and sanctions is problematic.

The problem of causal order also plagues the perception/self-report studies (e.g., Waldo and Chiricos, 1972; Silberman, 1976). In these studies, surveyed individuals' self-reported delinquencies are related to the same individuals' perceptions of likely sanctions. If the dominant direction of influence is from perception of sanctions to behavior, then deterrence hypotheses may be addressed. If, on the other hand, the predominant influence is from behavior to perceptions, as one might expect from conforming individuals' overestimating the efficiency and severity of the criminal justice system (Jensen, 1969; Claster, 1967; Walker, 1965), then the question of deterrence is not addressed. Because these studies usually relate *present* perceptions to reports of *past* behavior the latter interpretation is perhaps more likely. Tittle (1977) attempted to resolve this dilemma by using self-reports of anticipated *future* behavior in certain hypothetical situations, but acknowledge the limitations of this approach. Therefore, these perception/self-report surveys, like the official data studies, do not provide resolution of the dominant direction of influence, and authors have generally had to depend on an untested assumption of causal directionality.[1]

The second major problem, contingency, refers to the need for specification of the variables which influence the existence and strength of deterrent effects. Tittle and Logan (1973:365) identified this problem clearly:

> At this point we can safely say only that sanctions apparently have some deterrent effect under some circumstances. It is now necessary to undertake careful research in an attempt to specify the conditions under which sanctions are likely to be important influences on behavior.

An extensive list of variables considered important has been proposed and sporadically examined. In addition to the classical considerations of certainty, severity, and swiftness, for example, Andenaes (1966) has proposed a *mala per se/mala quia prohibita* distinction; Chambliss (1967) has suggested an expressive/instrumental dichotomy and a commitment-to-crime-as-a-way-of-life continuum; others have suggested distinctions between deterrent effects and moralizing or educational effects of sanctions (Zimring and Hawkins, 1973), between formal and informal sanctions (Anderson et al., forthcoming, a), between crimes against persons and other crimes (Silberman, 1976), between existence and perceptions of sanctions (Waldo and Chiricos, 1972), and so on. Indeed, the proliferation of such distinctions, though necessary for adequate conceptualization of complex phenomena, may have inhibited efforts to develop a more comprehensive theory of crime.

This leads to the third major problem in deterrence, the absence of theoretical integration. Most deterrence research seems to imply that deterrence variables operate in a social vacuum, independent of other influences. However,

> Were we to incorporate the notion of deterrence, we might move toward closure in our current theories. . . . Perhaps the missing link is fear of sanction. If we knew more about the conditions under which people come to perceive and fear sanctions, we might be able to account for these negative instances [in which people "differentially associate" but do not become criminals, and so forth]. [Tittle and Rowe, 1974:461]

Although this lack of theoretical integration has been noted by Tittle and Rowe (1974) and Wellford (1974), to date only Meier and Johnson (1977) have attempted to unite deterrence with some broader theory of criminal behavior. Their contribution was to acknowledge deterrence as one form of social control, simultaneously considering legal and extralegal influences. In the present paper, this perspective is extended and systematically applied in a recursive theoretical model.

CONTROL THEORY

To attempt an integration of deterrence and control theory, it is appropriate to first consider the background assumptions

(Gouldner, 1970) which underlie each, in order to assess the likely compatibility of the two perspectives. The most important of these background assumptions (and for our purposes, the only important one) is the nature of man.

Other theories—theories of "strain" or "cultural deviance" (see Hirschi, 1969:1-16)—assume conformity and try to explain deviance by positing some sort of extraordinary circumstances. By so doing, they tend to evoke an oversocialized conception of man (Wrong, 1961; see also Ellis, 1971) which virtually precludes the possibility of deviance. Control theory, on the other hand, adopts an image of man in which self-interest is assumed, and self-serving deviance is nonproblematic. For control theories, the Hobbesian question—Why do men obey the rules of society?—is central. " 'Why do they do it?' is simply not the question the theory is designed to answer. The question is, 'Why don't we do it' " (Hirschi, 1969:34).

In the classical writings on deterrence (especially those of Bentham) man is seen as not only hedonistic but also essentially rational. However, it is not necessary to endorse a rigid Benthamite moral calculus in order to suggest that men are sometimes influenced by calculations of expected gain or loss. For present purposes, it is sufficient to simply note that control theory and deterrence share an essentially hedonistic image of man.

In control theory, this hedonism is restrained primarily by the individual's relationship to the larger society (Hirschi, 1969). In deterrence theory, it is restrained by fear of sanction. It should be possible, therefore, to combine the restraining influences of social solidarity and rational fear of consequences into a single theoretical perspective. Accordingly, we will modify Hirschi's (1969) control theory by adding "fear of sanctions" as an additional element of the bond to society and by specifying the resulting relationships in a recursive model.

Hirschi's original model posited that "Delinquent acts occur when an individual's bond to society is weak or broken" (Hirschi, 1969:16). Four elements of this bond to society were then specified: The affective *attachment* to conventional others, a rational *commitment* to (or stake in) conformity, a time-consuming *involvement* in conventional activities, and a *belief* in the personal legitimacy of the law. Hirschi's (1969) analysis and Hindelang's (1973) replication both found empirical support for the salience of each element of the bond, though Hirschi (1969) questioned the conceptual adequacy of involvement.

Although Hirschi (1969) did not present his theory in the form of a recursive causal model, we can use his discussion of the relations among the elements to place the theory in this form. Figure 1 identifies the major causal sequences proposed or implied in Hirschi's theory.

In Hirschi's model, delinquency is directly influenced by each of the elements of the bond. In addition there are paths of influence from attachment to commitment to involvement and from attachment to belief. The influence of attachment on commitment, for example, is suggested in these statements: "Students with weak affectional ties to parents also tend to have little concern for the opinion of teachers and tend not to like school" (Hirschi, 1969:131). More specifically, "the causal chain runs from academic incompetence to poor school performance to disliking of school to rejection of the school's authority to the commission of delinquent acts" (Hirschi, 1969:132). Involvement, in turn, was seen as a consequence of commitment. "Such activities are presumably in large part consequences of such commitment...." (Hirschi, 1969:191). Finally, belief was seen as a consequence of attachment: "The chain of causation is thus from attachment to parents, through concern for the approval of persons in positions of authority, to

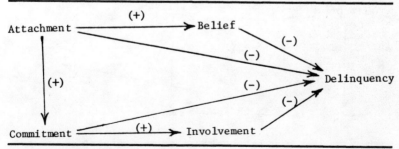

Figure 1: HIRSCHI'S CAUSAL MODEL.

belief that the rules of society are binding on one's conduct" (Hirschi, 1969:200).

Hirschi acknowledged other examples of covariation between elements of the bond, but the above relationships are the only ones for which his statements justify an assertion of causal order.

One of the major advantages of a simple recursive causal model is that it forces specification of such relationships. A related disadvantage, however, is that feedback loops and reciprocal relations are denied, thus oversimplifying complex phenomena. In the formulation we are about to propose, however, the advantages of clearly specified relationships are held to outweigh the disadvantages of oversimplification, and a recursive format is used.

The model we propose (Figure 2) is a combination of deterrence and Hirsch's control theory, adding "fear of sanctions" as an element of the bond to society and deleting "involvement." "Fear," as used herein, refers to the individual's perception of formal and informal sanctions likely to be attendant on his violation of law. Variables intended to measure involvement (church attendance, memberships in formal organizations) were too conceptually ambiguous to be of theoretic utility, since they could also be considered measures of attachment and/or commitment. For this reason, and because of the theoretical weakness of this variable (Hirschi, 1969:188-191), involvement has been deleted from the model.

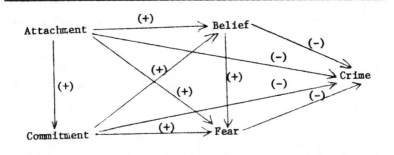

Figure 2: THE PRESENT MODEL

The causal order proposed for the components of the model is as follows: Attachment, commitment, belief, fear, crime. In this sequence, each element is influenced by each element which precedes it, and in turn influences each element which follows. Belief, for example, is influenced by attachment and commitment, and in turn influences fear and crime. All of the relations among the four elements of the bond (attachment, commitment, belief, fear) are hypothesized to be positive. The effect of each element on crime is hypothesized to be negative.

The causal order posited in the model is not the only possible sequence, and its rationale requires elaboration. Attachment is posited as the exogenous variable in this model both on the basis of temporal priority and dominant influence. Concern for the opinion of others (especially family) begins early in life and affects the other elements of the bond. For example, attachment to work or school leads to a commitment to those institutions. If one doesn't like his job, the possibility of losing it is less threatening. Attachments to family, church, school, or other conventional institutions tends to foster a belief in the legitimacy of those institutions and in the law which supports them. Attachment to others should also influence one's perceptions of sanctions (fear), especially informal sanctions. Sensitivity to the opinions of conventional others should inhibit crime.

One's commitments should both enhance one's belief in the legitimacy of the legal order and, since one has more to lose, heighten the fear of sanctions. Crime, of course, would threaten one's stake in conformity.

Belief affects crime both directly and through its effect on fear of sanctions. According to Jensen (1969), those who support the law also tend to overestimate the penalties for its infraction.

Finally, the fear of punishment is hypothesized to have a direct influence on crime.

The rationale for some of these hypothesized associations is obviously weaker than for others. By beginning with the full model, however, we are prepared to give the data more complete consideration. Based on the results of the analysis, the model is subject to revision.

RESEARCH METHODS

This study is based on data from personal interviews with 274 randomly selected white adults in Tallahassee, Florida. Utilizing self-reported criminality and perceptions of sanctions, the study thus shares most of the same general strengths and weaknesses of other similar studies in deterrence (Waldo and Chiricos, 1972; Silberman, 1976).

The advantages of this approach include the focusing of theoretic interest at the individual level, the consideration of *perceptions* of sanctions (rather than mere statutory provisions for them), the nonreliance on official data, and avoidance of the problems of aggregated data (Cartwright, 1969:184; Cousineau, 1973). The principal problems with this approach are the difficulty of soliciting sensitive information, the questionable validity of self-reports, and the representativeness of the sample surveyed.

The problems associated with the perception/self-report approach, however, may be minimized through careful planning and execution of research. For example, a carefully designed interview schedule, believable assurances of anonymity or confidentiality, and skilled interviewing can do much to overcome respondents' resistance to reveal sensitive information.

The validity of self-reports has been assessed by comparison of known groups (Nye and Short, 1957; Voss, 1963), comparison of self-reports with official records (Farrington, 1973, for example) or informants' reports (Gold, 1966), and by polygraph (Clark and Tifft, 1966). Although these studies have not shown self-reports to be superior to official data (Nettler, 1973), self-reports do at least provide a more extensive index of criminal involvement. Several studies (Hirschi, 1969:64; Voss, 1963; Nettler, 1973:96-97) have found that the major conclusions of their analyses (i.e., the social locations of crime) were unaffected by the decision to use self-reports or official data.

A third problem of other self-report/perception studies of deterrence has been the reliance on samples of college students for data (Waldo and Chiricos, 1972; Silberman, 1976), thus raising questions about the generality of their findings. The present study, however, differs from this pattern in two respects. First, it is a study of *adults* (18-50) rather than juveniles or students. Second, the survey population is adults residing in a given *community* rather than in an institutional (e.g., reformatory) or quasi-institutional setting (e.g., college).

The population sampled, then, consisted of white adults, 18 to 50 years old, residing in noninstitutional settings in Tallahassee, Florida. Blacks were excluded from the sample because no black interviewers were available. This increases the sensitivity of the analysis but limits the generalizability of the findings.

A two stage sampling procedure was used. First a systematic random sample of residential addresses was selected from the Tallahassee City Directory. Then within each household, the respondent to be interviewed was selected by a random sampling table similar to that used by Ennis (1967).

Although several researchers (Krohn et al., 1974; Gold, 1970; Hardt and Bodine, 1965; Kulik et al., 1968) have suggested that anonymity may be less important for self-report studies than previously thought, several respondents during the pretests expressed strong reservations about giving their names or about giving personal information when names had been recorded. Consequently, during the survey, names were not taken; respondents were told that their selection was random and that no identifying information would be recorded. Although certain information (age, sex, address, phone number) would have made possible the surreptitious identification of most respondents, the pledge of anonymity was honored. This precluded a measure of external validation (i.e., self-reported arrests versus police-recorded arrests). However, because the data were collected through interviews, interviewers were able to detect erratic responses, obvious inconsistencies, and some deliberate concealment or exaggeration. On these bases, five interviews (2%) were excluded from the analysis; 23 others (8%) were considered suspect in minor respects, but were not excluded.

Having sketched the major outlines of the study, we may now consider the operationalization of key concepts. Although multiple measures of each element of the bond are available in the data, the analysis to follow is based on those indices or single variables found to be conceptually and empirically most relevant for the model.[2]

An *attachment index* was created by counting the number of maximally favorable responses from eight interview items: the importance of having one's spouse's (children's, mother's, father's) approval, one's approval of his friends, perceived dependability of friends, and one's liking of school and/or his job. The attachment index thus measures one's attachment to family, friends, school, and work.

The operationalization of commitment for this analysis presented particular problems, since an ordinal correlation analysis (Minor, 1975) had revealed small but complex and inconsistent relationships between commitment and crime. Several commitment variables (e.g., likelihood of promotion, head of household, commitment index[3]), contrary to theory, were *positively* related to crime, though these relationships were usually reduced below significance when age and sex were controlled. Other indicators of commitment (e.g., length of employment), whose zero-order relationships with crime were supportive of the theory, were similarly confounded with age. Ultimately, the only commitment variables with consistent, nonspurious negative relations to crime were measures of social status: income and occupational status. For the following analysis, income is used as the single indicator of commitment.

The third element of the bond in our model—belief—was measured by the belief index, a Likert scale formed from four items addressing one's belief in the legitimacy of the law.[4]

The last element of the bond—fear—was measured by responses to a series of hypothetical situations.[5] These responses provided measures of perceived certainty, severity, swiftness of punishment, and of anticipated informal sanctions from family and friends. A correlation analysis revealed that perceptions of severity and swiftness had no apparent effect on crime, but certainty and the informal sanctions were negatively associated with crime, as expected. Since our primary interest in fear concerns the deterrent effect of formal sanctions, the perception of certainty of sanction is the operationalization of fear used in the following analysis.

Self-reports provide six measures of criminality: the frequency of five specific offenses (speeding, drunk driving, smoking marijuana, shoplifting, and tax fraud) and a frequency index for total criminality, based on 31 offenses.

ANALYSIS

Because we are interested in developing specific causal models, this analysis utilizes interval statistics. We must thus justify interval treatment of these data. First, except for fear of sanctions, all of the variables used in the analysis are either interval (age, specific offenses), dichotomous (sex), or have a large number of categories (attachment, income, belief, frequency), legitimating interval treatment (Reynolds, 1974). Second, interval treatment of ordinal data usually does not bias the analysis (Labovitz, 1967, 1970; Boyle, 1970). Third, for the present data, the relevant interval and ordinal statistics, r and tau, are generally similar, as Table 1 indicates. The few exceptions to this, and their effects on interpretation of the data, will be discussed in the specific analyses.

The path diagrams which follow are based on a foreward selection stepwise regression procedure (see Nie et al., 1975), terminated when the standardized regression coefficients (beta weights) of any additional variables would be less than .10. Put simply, only paths of .10 or larger are included.

Although the analyses have been conducted for each of the separate measures of crime identified above, path diagrams will be presented only for those instances in which the model has notable explanatory power. In the other cases, we will be more concerned with the reasons for the model's failure than with explication of the specific paths of (slight) influence.

Speeding, Driving Under the Influence. For each of these two offenses, the model accounts for only about 5% of the variance. Even when age and sex are added to the model (as uncorrelated exogenous variables), the R^2 is raised only to .09 or .10. Moreover, contrary to expectation, in each case the variable of fear is eliminated from the model because the relevant path coefficient is less than .10.

Table 1. CORRELATION MATRIX COMPARING Tau AND r

	Attachment Age	Sex	Attachment Index	Commitment (Income)	Belief Index	Fear (Certainty)	Speeding	DUI	Marijuana	Shop-lifting	Tax Fraud	Frequency
Age	1.00	.07	.22	.21	.25	.10	−.19	−.20	−.35	−.19	.04	−.34
Sex	.07	1.00	.19	−.05	.15	.25	−.15	−.32	−.11	−.05	−.16	−.24
Attachment Index	.28	.21	1.00	.15	.34	.24	−.15	−.21	−.29	−.22	−.06	−.29
Commitment (Income)	.23	−.06	.21	1.00	.18	.02	.02	−.02	−.22	−.18	.01	−.10
Belief Index	.35	.18	.41	.17	1.00	.27	−.16	−.23	−.39	−.23	−.04	−.33
Fear (Certainty)	.19	.32	.31	.02	.37	1.00	−.14	−.30	−.25	−.11	−.19	−.27
Speeding	−.22	−.13	−.13	.12	−.15	−.10	1.00	.24	.20	.13	.16	.45
DUI	−.17	−.22	−.14	−.01	−.22	−.11	.21	1.00	.43	.20	.12	.55
Marijuana	−.31	−.10	−.25	−.15	−.47	−.17	.09	.33	1.00	.36	.03	.52
Shoplifing	−.12	.00	−.12	−.11	−.22	−.09	.01	.10	.51	1.00	−.09	.27
Tax Fraud	.01	−.15	−.07	.01	−.03	−.24	.14	.12	−.02	−.05	1.00	.29
Frequency	−.44	−.29	−.35	−.05	−.48	−.36	.43	.49	.68	.38	.27	1.00

NOTE: N = 260. Tau is above the diagonal, r below. The critical levles for statistical significance for tau and r are as follows:

	$p < .05$	$p < .01$	$p < .001$
tau	.07	.10	.14
r	.10	.15	.18

These unexpected findings may be clarified by both methodological and theoretical considerations. First consider the deletion of fear from the models. For speeding, this deletion is apparently a result of multicollinearity, since there is a slight zero-order association between fear and speeding (tau = -.14, p < .001).

The exclusion of fear from the model for driving under the influence is especially surprising, since previous studies (Ross, Campbell, and Glass, 1970) had shown a deterrent effect for this offense, and an ordinal correlation analysis of the present data had indicated a moderate association (tau = -.30) between fear and driving after drinking. However, because the interval measure of association is much smaller (r = -.11), this effect is not revealed in the path analysis. For the present, this finding must remain ambiguous.[6]

Substantively, we suspect that small R^2s may result because our model is simply ill-suited to such nonstigmatizing, habitual, or situationally induced behaviors as speeding and drunk driving, behaviors which Ross (1961) called "folk crime." For such offenses it may be necessary to take into account the specific contexts within which the behaviors occur in order to develop models for these particular offenses.

Marijuana Use. A very parsimonious model (Figure 3) indicates that belief in the legitimacy of the law accounts for 22% of the variance in marijuana use. It might be argued that both belief and marijuana use are functions of age, and that the relation between belief and marijuana use is spurious. This does not seem to be the case, however: Age alone accounts for only 9% of the variance in marijuana use ($R^2 = .094$), and increases the explanatory power of the restricted model by only about 2% ($R^2 = .243$ versus .220).[7] Thus the effect of age on marijuana use is largely mediated through belief, but the effect of belief is not explained by the association between belief and age.

Shoplifting. The model for shoplifting explains only 5% of the variance, and fear is again eliminated from the model. The weakness of the model in this case is probably due to the rarity of the offense, since only 17 of 274 respondents admitted

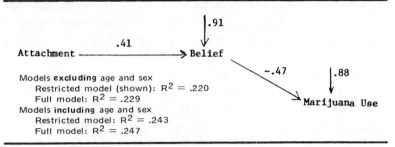

Figure 3: PATH DIAGRAM FOR SMOKING MARIJUANA

shoplifting in the past year. Nevertheless, if the present model is accurate, the elimination of fear does not necessarily contradict Cameron's (1954) finding that most shoplifters are effectively deterred from subsequent offenses after being caught. Her data suggest the efficacy of *specific* deterrence for shoplifting; the present data (if confirmed) would suggest the ineffectiveness of *general* deterrence for shoplifting.

Cheating on Taxes. Tax fraud is directly influenced only by fear of sanction, which accounts for 6% of the variance. In light of previous research linking moral obligation and tax compliance (Schwartz and Orleans, 1967), the absence of a direct path from belief to tax fraud is surprising. However, the number of tax cheaters (34) in the present sample may be too small for the detection of weak influences or adequate representation of paths of influence. That is, the larger and more heterogenous the nonoffender group becomes, the less sensitive comparisons between offenders and nonoffenders will be (von Hirsch, 1976:22; Gottfredson, 1967:176).

Frequency of Crime. In four of the five preceding crime-specific analyses, the model accounted for only about 5% of the variance in the dependent variable. Two of these offenses (speeding and driving after drinking) were classified as "folk crimes," to which the model may be ill-suited. The absence of a deterrent effect for these offenses was surprising, however, especially since an ordinal correlation analysis had indicated the presence of such an effect. In the other two cases (shoplifting and tax fraud), the numbers of offenders were too small for dependable analysis. Only in the case of marijuana use did the crime-specific analysis seem adequate, and there virtually all of the explanatory power was concentrated in a single variable, belief.

The explanatory power of the model for crime in general ($R^2 = .29$) is much better than it is for any of the specific offenses (See Figure 4), and interpretation of this model is less confounded by the problems which bias the crime-specific models: Small numbers of offenders, multicollinearity, and discrepancies between ordinal and interval measures of association. Thus, although crime-specific models are theoretically desirable, the path analysis presented in Figure 4 provides a more reliable examination of the model. As Silberman (1976:445) has noted, "we may be able to predict generalized patterns of deviance better than specific deviant acts."

According to this analysis, crime is directly influenced by each element of the bond except commitment. Although all of the paths from commitment (i.e., to belief, fear, and crime) are deleted in accordance with our decision rule, all of the paths from the other elements of the bond remain intact. This restricted model accounts for 29% of the variance in crime, or 37% if age and sex are added to the model.

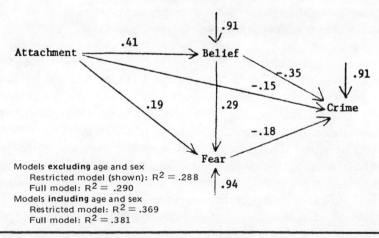

Figure 4: PATH DIAGRAM FOR THE FREQUENCY OF CRIMINAL BEHAVIOR

DISCUSSION

We have argued that the three major problems in deterrence research and theory are contingency, causal order, and theoretical integration. The contingency of deterrence relationships has been analyzed for the present data (Minor, 1975), but because space limitations preclude the elaboration of those findings here, they will be the subject of another paper. In this paper, a specific causal order has been assumed, but not demonstrated. Demonstration of causal sequence would require either longitudinal study or experimental method, since statistical efforts to resolve causal order are unsatisfactory (Heise, 1970).

In this paper we have assumed a specific causal sequence in order to propose and examine a theoretical integration of control theory and deterrence. Such an integration is required to overcome atomistic conceptualizations of the processes involved in conformity and deviance.

The data for this examination were obtained from a random sample of white adults in a southern city. Because of the nature of the sample, the findings should be more generalizable than those of other perception/self-report studies which have been based on student samples or institutionalized youths.

To consider the theoretical integration proposed, we have relied on the technique of path analysis, for two primary reasons. First, path analysis enables the examination of the empirical consequences of a proposed *system* of relationships, rather than mere pairwise consideration of relations among variables (Land, 1969; Duncan, 1966). Second, path analysis enables consideration of the consequences of deleting certain paths or variables.[8]

Gibbs (1975) has argued that theories of deterrence may need to be crime-specific, that is, different depending on the type of crime. This is a laudable theoretic goal, especially for folk crimes, white-collar crimes, and other types of offenses to which most contemporary theories seem ill-suited. On the other hand, some of the practical limitations of such an approach must be acknowledged. In both Silberman's (1976) analysis and the present study, the theoretical formulations were better able to explain generalized patterns of deviance than the incidence of specific offenses. Moreover, recent reviews of typological efforts in criminology have questioned their empirical adequacy (Amos and Wellford, 1973; Gibbons, 1975).

Based on these general patterns of criminality revealed in this study, then, the model we propose for future research is that presented in Figure 4: Attachment to belief to fear to crime, with all paths included. A few comments are in order concerning this model.

Two of the variables in Hirschi's original model, involvement and commitment, have been deleted. Hirschi (1969) noted the persistent confounding of involvement with other elements of the bond and the implicit erroneous assumption that delinquent behavior was very time consuming. These arguments are persuasive to us, and we feel no need to include involvement in the model we propose.

The tentative elimination of commitment is a more difficult decision, since both Hirschi (1969) and Hindelang (1973) found empirical support for this element of the bond. As we have seen in the present analysis, however, in a multivariate framework virtually all of the slight explanatory power of commitment is absorbed by other elements of the bond, due to multicollinearity. Moreover, even considering only zero-order associations between crime and several measures of commitment, only slight and inconsistent relationships are evident (Minor, 1975).

The resulting model, then, has crime dependent on attachment, fear and belief, reflecting three major dimensions of social theory. The first of these is the Durkheimian notion that conformity is induced through a sense of social solidarity. Certainly attachment to conventional others or institutions is a measure of this social solidarity. The second dimension is a rational evaluation of consequences, which is explicit in Bentham's work and implicit in exchange and learning theories. Fear of sanction reflects this dimension. Finally, the third element, belief in the personal legitimacy of the law, seems to address another important dimension—that of the congruence between professed attitudes and exhibited behavior. (See Liska, 1974, for an overview of the attitude-behavior consistency controversy.)

Nevertheless, there is at least one important determinant of crime which is not included in this model. If conformity is a consequence of the social bond, then crime may occur when these bonds are neutralized (Sykes and Matza, 1957), episodically released (Matza, 1964), or overcome by situational inducements (Briar and Piliaven, 1965) or aleatory risks (Short and Strodtbeck, 1965). The model we have proposed does not specifically include these situational inducements and neutralizations. If it did, and if a way were found to adequately measure these variables, the theory would likely be strengthened.

NOTES

1. One study, not yet published, resolves this problem by using panel data. See Anderson et al. (forthcoming, b).

2. Such ex post facto selection of variables (i.e., after reconsidering conceptual adequacy and examining correlations) has the effect of maximizing the theoretical and mathematical explanatory power of the model.

3. The commitment index was created in the same manner as the attachment index, by counting the number of maxima on eight indicators of investment: head of household, relative ability at one's job or at school, likelihood of promotion, threat of arrest to one's job (workers), job prospects (students) or continued education (students), and one's diligence at tasks undertaken.

4. "I feel a strong moral obligation to obey the law." "Sometimes people get into situations where they have to break the law, even if they don't want to." "If you have a problem, the law won't help you unless you have a lot of money." "People should always obey the law, even if they disagree with it."

5. For example, one measure of perceived certainty was provided by responses to the following question. "Suppose you were driving home after having too much to drink at a party. Do you think you would get caught by the police . . . almost all of the time, three-fourths of the time, half of the time, one-fourth of the time, or almost none of the time?"

6. This difference, between tau = −.30 and r = −.11, is the largest discrepancy in Table 1. Because the perceived certainty of punishment for specific offenses is measured at only five levels, it seems more appropriate to treat this relationship as ordinal and accept the deterrence interpretation. Nevertheless, because these data do not provide a consistent interpretation, the issue requires additional data for resolution.

7. In Figures 3 and 4, the explanatory power (R^2) of four versions of the model is provided, to clarify the empirical consequences of alternative formulations. Note that in Figure 3 the inclusion of age and sex as uncorrelated exogenous variables (r = .07, n.s.) does not greatly improve the model's explanatory power. However, the inclusion of age and sex in the model for crime frequency (Figure 4) does make a substantial difference. In each case, the "full model" includes the direct effects of all

variables on crime, the "restricted model" includes only those paths greater than
±.10.

8. Gibbs (1975) suggests that exploratory research in deterrence, or more properly in general prevention, should seek the elimination of unnecessary variables.

REFERENCES

AMOS, W.E., and WELLFORD, C.F. (1973). "Typologies and treatment." Pp. 176-215 in J. Cull and R. Hardy, Fundamentals of criminal behavior and correctional systems. Springfield: Thomas.

ANDERSON, L.S., CHIRICOS, T.G., and WALDO, G.P. (forthcoming, a). "Formal and informal sanctions: A comparison of deterrent effects." Social Problems.

ANDERSON, L.S., WALDO, G.P., and CHIRICOS, T.G. (forthcoming, b). "A longitudinal approach to the study of deterrence." Paper to be presented at the 1977 annual meeting of the American Sociological Association.

ANDENAES, J. (1966). "The general preventive effects of punishment." University of Pennsylvania Law Review, 114:949-983.

BOWERS, W.J. (1974). Executions in America. Lexington, Mass.: D.C. Heath.

BOWERS, W.J., and SALEM, R.G. (1972). "Severity of formal sanctions as a repressive response to deviant behavior." Law and Society Review, 6:427-441.

BOYLE, R.P. (1970). "Path analysis and ordinal data." American Journal of Sociology, 75:461-480.

BRIAR, S., and PILIAVEN, I. (1965). "Delinquency, situational inducements, and commitment to conformity." Social Problems, 13:35-45.

CAMERON, M.O. (1954). The booster and the snitch. New York: Free Press.

CAMPBELL, D.T., and ROSS, H.L. (1968). "The Connecticut crackdown on speeding: Time-series data in quasi-experimental analysis." Law and Society Review, 3:33-53.

CARTWRIGHT, D.S. (1969). "Ecological variables." Pp. 155-218 in E.F. Borgatta (ed.), Sociological methodology 1969. San Francisco: Jossey-Bass.

CHAMBLISS, W.J. (1967). "Types of deviance and the effectiveness of legal sanctions." Wisconsin Law Review, 67:703-719.

CLARK, J.P., and TIFFT, L.L. (1966). "Polygraph and interview validation of self-reported deviant behavior." American Sociological Review, 31:516-523.

CLASTER, D.S. (1967). "Comparison of risk perception between delinquents and non-delinquents." Journal of Criminal Law, Criminology, and Police Science, 58:80-86.

COUSINEAU, D.F. (1973). "A critique of the ecological approach to the study of deterrence." Social Science Quarterly, 54:152-158.

DUNCAN, O.D. (1966). "Path analysis: Sociological examples." American Journal of Sociology, 72:1-16.

ELLIS, D.P. (1971). "The Hobbesian problem of order: A critical appraisal of the normative solution." American Sociological Review, 36:692-703.

ENNIS, P.H. (1967). Criminal Victimization in the United States: A report of a National Survey. Report submitted to the President's Commission on Law Enforcement and Administration of Justice. Washington, D.C.: U.S. Government Printing Office.

FARRINGTON, D.P. (1973). "Self-reports of deviant behavior: Predictive and stable?" Journal of Criminal Law and Criminology, 64:99-110.

GIBBONS, D.C. (1975). "Offender typologies—two decades later." British Journal of Criminology, 15:140-156.

GIBBS, J.P. (1968). "Crime, punishment, and deterrence." Southwestern Social Science Quarterly, 48:515-530.

——— (1975). Crime, punishment, and deterrence. New York: Elsevier.

GOLD, M. (1966). "Undetected delinquent behavior." Journal of Research in Crime and Delinquency, 3:27-46.

——— (1970). Delinquent behavior in an American city. Belmont, Calif.: Wadsworth.

GOTTFREDSON, D.M. (1967). "Assessment and prediction methods in crime and deliquency." P. 171-187 of President's Commission on Law Enforcement and Administration of Justice, Task Force Report: Juvenile Delinquency and Youth Crime. Washington, D.C.: U.S. Government Printing Office.

GOULDNER, A.W. (1970). The coming crisis of Western sociology. New York: Basic Books.

HARDT, R.H., and BODINE, G.E. (1965). Development of self-report instruments in delinquency research: A conference report. Syracuse, N.Y.: Youth Development Center, Syracuse University.

HEISE, D.R. (1970). "Causal inference from panel data." Pp. 3-27 in E.F. Borgatta and G.W. Bohrnstedt (eds.), Sociological methodology 1970. San Francisco: Jossey-Bass.

HINDELANG, M.J. (1973). "Causes of delinquency: A partial replication and extension." Social Problems, 20:471-487.

HIRSCHI, T. (1969). Causes of delinquency. Berkeley: University of California Press.

JENSEN, G.F. (1969). " 'Crime doesn't pay': Correlates of a shared misunderstanding." Social Problems, 17:189-201.

KROHN, M., WALDO, G.P., and CHIRICOS, T.G. (1974). "Self-reported delinquency: A comparison of structured interviews and self-administered checklists." Journal of Criminal Law and Criminology, 65:545-553.

KULIK, J.A., STEIN, K.B., and SARBIN, T.R. (1968). "Disclosure of delinquent behavior under conditions of anonymity and nonanonymity." Journal of Counseling and Clinical Psychology, 32:506-509.

LABOVITZ, S. (1967). "Some observations on measurement and statistics." Social Forces, 46:151-160.

——— (1970). "The assignment of numbers to rank order categories." American Sociological Review, 35:515-524.

LAND, K.C. (1969). "Principles of path analysis." Pp. 3-37 in E.F. Borgatta (ed.), Sociological methodology 1969. San Francisco: Jossey-Bass.

LISKA, A.E. (1974). "Emergent issues in the attitude-behavior consistency controversy." American Sociological Review, 39:261-272.

MATZA, D. (1964). Delinquency and drift. New York: John Wiley.

MEIER, R.F., and JOHNSON, W.T. (1977). "Deterrence as social control: The legal and extralegal production of conformity." American Sociological Review, 42:292-304.

MINOR, W.W. (1975). Control theory and deterrence of crime: A theoretical and empirical integration. Unpublished Ph.D. dissertation, Florida State University.

NETTLER, G. (1973). Explaining crime. New York: McGraw-Hill.

NIE, N.H., HULL, C.H., JENKINS, J.G., STEINBRENNER, K., and BENT, D.H.

(1975). SPSS: Statistical package for the social sciences. New York: McGraw-Hill.
NYE, F.I., and SHORT, J.F., Jr. (1957). "Scaling delinquent behavior." American Sociological Review, 22:326-331.
REYNOLDS, H.T. (1974). "Nonparametric partial correlation and causal analysis." Sociological Methods and Research, 2:376-392.
ROSS, H.L. (1961). "Traffic law violation: A folk crime." Social Problems, 8:231-241.
ROSS, H.L., CAMPBELL, D.T., and GLASS, G.V. (1970). "Determining the social effects of a legal reform: The British 'Breathalyzer' crackdown of 1967." American Behavioral Scientist, 13:493-509.
SCHWARTZ, B. (1968). "The effect in Philadelphia of Pennsylvania's increased penalties for rape and attempted rape." Journal of Criminal Law, Criminology, and Police Science, 59:509-515.
SCHWARTZ, R.D., and ORLEANS, S. (1967). "On legal sanctions." University of Chicago Law Review, 34:274-300.
SHORT, J.R., Jr., and STRODTBECK, F.L. (1965). Group process and gang delinquency. Chicago: University of Chicago Press.
SILBERMAN, M. (1976). "Toward a theory of criminal deterrence." American Sociological Review, 41:442-461.
SYKES, G.M., and MATZA, D. (1957). "Techniques of neutralization: A theory of delinquency." American Journal of Sociology, 22:664-670.
TITTLE, C.R. (1969). "Crime rates and legal sanctions." Social Problems, 16:409-423.
——— (1977). "Sanction fear and the maintenance of social order." Social Forces, (March):579-596.
TITTLE, C.R., and LOGAN, C.H. (1973). "Sanctions and deviance: Evidence and remaining questions." Law and Society Review, 7:371-392.
TITTLE, C.R., and ROWE, A.R. (1974). "Certainty of arrest and crime rates: A further test of the deterrence hypothesis." Social Forces, 52:455-462.
Von HIRSCH, A. (1976). Doing justice: The choice of punishments. New York: Hill and Wang.
VOSS, H.L. (1963). "Ethnic differentials in delinquency in Honolulu." Journal of Criminal Law, Criminology, and Police Science, 54:322-327.
WALDO, G.P., and CHIRICOS, T.G. (1972). "Perceived penal sanction and self-reported criminality: A neglected approach to deterrence research." Social Problems, 19:522-540.
WALKER, N. (1965). Crime and punishment in Britain. Chicago: Aldine.
——— (1971). Sentencing in a rational society. New York: Basic Books.
WELLFORD, C.F. (1974). "Deterrence: Issues and methodologies in the analysis of the impact of legal threat in crime control." Journal of Criminal Law and Criminology, 65:117-122.
WRONG, D. (1961). "The oversocialized conception of man in modern sociology." American Sociological Review, 26:183-198.
ZIMRING, F.E., and HAWKINS, G. (1973). Deterrence: The legal threat in crime control. Chicago: University of Chicago Press.

John P. Clark
Richard Hollinger
University of Minnesota

ON THE FEASIBILITY OF
EMPIRICAL STUDIES OF
WHITE-COLLAR CRIME

In 1964 Richard Quinney wrote that white-collar crime as an area of criminological study suffered from "undefined scope" and "little conceptual clarity" (Quinney, 1964). In the paper, he advocated a total reorientation of theory and research. According to Quinney, the critical problem with the concept of white-collar crime was that it covered such a "diverse set of behaviors" that there was little chance for the formulation of any systematic causal explanations of the phenomena which the term so vaguely represented.

In order to make progress concerning the ambiguity surrounding the "unit of analysis," Quinney suggested that we first abandon Sutherland's criteria of "respectability" and "upper socioeconomic class." Instead, he advocated reconceptualizing white-collar crime in terms of *occupational* crime. By occupational crime, Quinney meant "all violations that occur in the course of occupational activity" (Quinney, 1964:210). Essentially, this shift, with which many others since Quinney have also agreed, removes central interest from the social status of the offender and instead makes the locus of the social activity the primary issue. A look at the literature indicates that, in fact, the relationship of primary interest has been crime and occupation, not crime and upper social class. Even Sutherland (1949) chose not to illustrate his now famous book principally with examples of upper social class criminality, but instead concentrated on the violations of the corporate business community. Shifting the central focus of the investigation to the violations of the workplace was not the only suggestion which Quinney gave for improving the quality of theory and research in this area. Instead of restricting the unit of analysis to only occupational crime, he suggested that we instead use the broader concept, occupational deviance. In short, Quinney argued that we no longer limit our examination only to those behaviors which are criminal, but instead focus on all rule-breaking that applies to occupational behavior. As he writes:

> a shift to the concept of occupational deviance would allow researchers to investigate actual departures from occupational norms without having to rely upon the otherwise necessary inference that violations of legal norms are also deviations from occupational norms. [Quinney, 1964:210]

Quinney's attempt to extend the scope of criminology beyond the limits of the criminal code was not a new suggestion. Almost from the day that the subject of white-collar crime was introduced to the discipline (Sutherland, 1940) *the* focal theoretical issue has been a debate between the intellectual merits of a broadly defined sociological analysis and the legal limits of the criminal law (Tappan, 1947). Even earlier, Thorsten Sellin advocated a similar reorientation of focus in *Culture Conflict and Crime* published in 1938. But, just as Sellin's writings failed to significantly alter the discipline of criminology, the publication of Quinney's article in 1964 has apparently stimulated little interest in the subject of "occupational deviance." At the risk of being accused of "beating a dead horse" we concur that a broader-based sociological and social psychological study of deviance (which obviously includes violations of the criminal law) has more merit than the exclusive focus upon strictly criminal behavior alone. Occupational deviation offers the greater potential for understanding the relationships among occupational structure, practice, and deviations. It is the purpose of this paper to substantiate this assertion and demonstrate that empirical studies from this perspective are feasible and productive.

NORM VIOLATIONS IN THE OCCUPATIONAL MILIEU

If we were interested only in that group of deviant acts which are sanctioned as criminal, a cursory review of the criminal code will give us a list of illegal behaviors which are related to the occupational setting. However, using the criminal code by which to select the unit of analysis might indicate more about the political nature of the societal reaction system than the sociological characteristics of occupational deviance. In short, the criminal code is an eclectic list of differentially sanctioned behaviors—hardly a representative picture of the entire range of occupational deviations.

Since our intentions are to understand that broader group of deviant behaviors which occur as a function of occupational activity, then the problematic issue involves delineating what will be the unit of analysis. Relevant questions include, Which acts are deviant? and, From whose normative structure? In order to provide an answer to both the above, it is necessary to identify the applicable normative systems in the occupational setting.

In a complex social structure there exist a number of separate but interrelated normative systems which influence the behavior of individuals. The specific conduct norms which are relevant to the actor are largely dependent upon the locus of the behavior in question. When the individual shifts to a new social setting, his normative expectations are altered correspondingly. Given the possible number of social settings, a single act may be positively sanctioned, negatively sanctioned, or be treated as nonproblematic, depending upon its behavioral significance to the others in the same social situation. In other words, behaviors differ as to their normative salience dependent upon the particular social setting. Inasmuch as there are many social settings with differing behavioral expectations, the conduct rules of each comprises a separate but interrelated normative system. Specifically, in the case of the work setting, we have identified four rule-producing sources; namely, (1) society, (2) the formal work organization, (3) the occupational association, and (4) the work group subculture. In the following section we shall discuss these normative systems and their relationships to occupational deviance and crime.

Societal-Legal Norms. The most relevant segment of the societal normative system is that set of formalized conduct rules called the law. By law we mean a normative system which is supported by the power of a political state (Chambliss and Seidman, 1971:8-10). Laws which originate as the product of powerful interest groups (Quinney, 1970:43) come from a number of federal, state, and municipal sources, resulting in criminal and civil law, administrative regulations, and judicial interpretations. Violations of these "legalized" norms are formally sanctioned by means of fines and/or incarceration.

Although these legal norms are technically applicable to all, they may obviously be more salient to the lives of some persons than others. As an example, the law prohibiting theft applies to all; however, the law against embezzlement (a form of theft) is most salient to those individuals entrusted with large amounts of money or assets in the course of their occupational activities. Even though law may be the most ubiquitous element of social control, it does not constitute the universe of conduct rules. There are other sets of norms which are salient to specific social settings and groups.

Norms of the Formal Work Organization. Within specific social settings we find rules of conduct which are germane to that particular arena of activity; including schools, churches, welfare and recreational organizations. Another social setting which specifies rules of conduct for its members is the formal work organization. The work bureaucracy creates rules of conduct for its members in relation to the manner in which tasks are expected to be completed. Those behaviors which are interpreted by those in power as inconsistent with the legitimate goals of the formal organization may be sanctioned as deviant. Depending on the seriousness, the bureaucracy may establish an internal sanctioning body to react to this deviant activity. Those employees judged as deviant can be sanctioned by means of a variety of techniques, including re-training, transfer, promotion, isolation, or dismissal.

The example of embezzlement which we used above as an instance of societal-legal norm violation can also be sanctioned as deviant from the point of view of the formal work organization. For not only is embezzlement a crime, but the unauthorized taking of money by employees is also inconsistent with the bureaucratic goals. The fact that a trusted employee has been detected stealing from the company is a serious threat to the integrity of the work organization. If sanctions are not immediately forthcoming from the bureaucracy, what is to deter other employees from attempting the same thing? For this reason, many organizations will often opt for internal sanctions as a response to deviance rather than invoking the criminal law (Robin, 1967). Thus, a theft which is technically a criminal matter is sanctioned also by management because of the importance of the act to the formal work organization.

On the other hand, there are situations in which we find the formal work organization encouraging violations of the law, rather than sanctioning them. In other words, there are times when the normative expectations of the work organization are *in*consistent with society's laws. As an example of this, let us take the case of industrial espionage. Stealing trade secrets from other organizations can most certainly be interpreted as a form of criminal theft. However, corporations who have encouraged this form of crime from their employees see this not as sanctionable deviance, but rather as consistent with the goal of insuring the continued viability of the business organization.

In sum, then, the formal organization provides a set of conduct rules for its employees. Violations of these rules, some of which may be crimes, are many times sanctioned internally by the formal work organization instead of (*or,* in addition to) the external sanctions of the criminal law. However, other organizational actions are directly in opposition to the letter of the criminal law. Thus, for some behaviors the rules of the formal work organization are consistent with the law; for others, obviously *in*consistent.

Norms of the Occupational Association. The norms of

society which have been codified in law and the rules of the formal work organization are not the only two sources of occupationally related conduct rules which are salient to the individual employee. Another source is the occupational association. We refer to the voluntary associations which transcend the geographical and bureaucratic boundaries of the workplace and link individuals of a single occupation who share the same occupational title in a different work organization. On the one hand, these occupational associations may unite kindred workers in order to share common experiences or grievances, like the labor union "local." On the other hand, we find the more formalized associations which provide the forum for establishing rules of conduct which certified practitioners of an occupation have agreed upon as minimally acceptable, as in the case of the American Bar Association, American Institute of Certified Public Accountants, and the American Medical Association. Dependent upon the potential negative ramifications for the membership, committees are established in order to sanction deviant members who threaten the "good name" of the entire occupation. For many workers these associations serve as the occupational reference group, in that sanctions such as censorship, fines, and/or expulsion from the association impute greater negative stigma than sanctions from any other source.

The accountant who has been adjudicated guilty of the crime of embezzlement not only has violated societal and formal work organizational rules, but he also risks being sanctioned by his occupational reference group, thereby jeopardizing his accreditation. The fact that this behavior directly contradicts the canons of the profession makes this act a serious affront to the practitioner's occupation and his peers. For some behaviors, then, it is the occupational association norms which provide the most salient constraints upon the activities of the worker.

The norms of the occupational association can also be in direct opposition to the law of society and the formal work organization. In the case of an illegal strike, for example, the norms of the occupational association—in this case the union—expect the worker to directly flaunt the rules of law and management in order to achieve worker demands.

In summary, the occupational association provides a set of conduct rules for its members. In some cases the sanctions for violations of these canons are more salient than the legal response because of the jeopardizing effect on the future career of the deviant. Alternatively, as we have noted before, under certain situations the occupational normative system may encourage direct violations of the law.

Norms of the Work Group. Thus far we have argued that employment norms are a collection of conduct rules promulgated by society, the formal work organization, and various occupational associations. Although the above normative systems certainly provide a repertoire of behavioral expectations, the most salient sets of norms may arise from the work group.

When individuals interact through direct communication in a particular social setting, patterns emerge which guide the conduct and clarify expectations of the participants. The work group—fellow workers who interact at the job setting on a day-to-day basis—abides by rules of conduct which routinize the interaction between individuals. These rules of behavior become a stabilizing factor against those deviant acts which threaten to disrupt or modify the existing order of the workplace. A number of case studies (e.g., Roethlisberger and Dickson, 1939; Bensman and Gerver, 1963; Horning, 1970) have documented the fact that the work group informally controls many aspects of the work experience directly in opposition to the wishes of management. Granted, not all work environments are identical in form and structure; nevertheless, we do find some semblance of the work group in most occupational environments. Whether as a member of a tight-knit shift team or merely as colleagues within the same department, employees interact with each other based upon a shared, informally established normative structure. Members of the work group whose acts and attitudes are inconsistent with group expectations are sanctioned by the majority as deviant. Techniques, such as gossip, ridicule, ostracism, exile, or in some cases physical violence, insure low levels of nonconformity within the work group.

For many acts the normative system of the work group will

be in concert with the societal-legal normative system. As an example we again use the case of the corporate embezzler. The theft of large amounts of the organization's money by a fellow worker may be informally sanctioned as unacceptable behavior by the rest of the work group. In fact, in many cases we expect it to be the work group who "tips-off" the proper authorities to the crime, thereby precipitating the apprehension of the deviant worker.

The norms of the work group are not always as consistent with the letter of the law, however. For other forms of theft, some of which may not be as flagrant as embezzlement—for example, expense account fraud—we may discover that these illegalities are consistent with the norms of the work group. In other words, some acts which are technically violations of the criminal law, not to mention inconsistent with management's rules, may oftentimes be supported and encouraged by the informal normative code of the work group.

In this section we have briefly outlined four separate but interrelated normative systems which apply to the occupational or work setting. The question of expressed interest to this paper concerns how a discussion of multiple normative systems in the employment milieu helps us to understand the relationship between crime and occupational conduct. We wish to argue that part of this answer lies in our understanding of a phenomenon we wish to call normative incongruity.

Normative Incongruity. As we have seen above, there is not always normative congruity between the various normative systems which apply to the work setting. The concept of normative incongruity is based upon the notion that for certain occupational behaviors we can identify conflicting interpretations as to whether a given act is an example of deviance *or* conformity. Although there are a number of possible configurations, we are most concerned with the extent of incongruity between society's criminal law and the other three normative systems.

A contemporary example might be illustrative of the theoretical ramifications of this concept. Recently, investigations into the finances of the Lockheed Aircraft Corporation have revealed extensive payments to foreign officials for the purpose of facilitating overseas sales of their aerospace products. The shockwaves from these revelations have shaken the foundations of governments and industry worldwide; the most turmoil being found in the countries of Japan, the Netherlands, and Italy, not to mention the United States. As a result of congressional investigations concerning these and other questionable practices, we now have documented that bribery is a standard operating procedure in the world of international trade. These payoffs and kickbacks seem to fly in the face of our cherished ideals of competition and free enterprise. In the last session of Congress, the Senate passed legislation sponsored by Senator William Proxmire (Democrat; Wisconsin) that if eventually made law would make illegal any payments or bribes by U.S. corporations to facilitate sales of their products.

The "Lockheed scandal" is an excellent example of normative incongruity. While the norms of society seem to indicate that bribery is behavior which is generally inconsistent with an open and free market, the norms of the formal work organization, occupational associations, and work groups either covertly or overtly are not in agreement. The almost endless stream of corporate testimony seems to indicate that payoffs and bribes are (a) the only way of doing business overseas, (b) have been going on for years, and (c) are functional for the businesses involved. In other words, the work environment argues for the behaviors to continue; at the same time, society is passing laws to prevent them.

What is important theoretically about the Lockheed example is that many other instances of occupational deviance and crime document similar manifestations of normative incongruity (e.g., the 1961 Electrical Industry Anti-Trust Conspiracy; Geis, 1967; Smith, 1961). Since we believe that normative incongruity is a critical factor in understanding occupational deviance and crime, let us explore in propositional form some potential research topics.

Proposition One: The degree of normative incongruity will determine the scope and content of *society's reaction* to the occupational deviance in question.

We predict that the societal reaction to behaviors which are supported by the various normative systems of the workplace will be shaped to a great extent by the degree of incongruity that is present. The greater the degree of incongruity, then, the more specific the law, the more severe the sentences, and the more concentrated will be the enforcement effort. Alternatively, we should not at all be surprised if attempts at legislating away this form of deviance are relatively ineffective due to the lack of agreement between legal norms and the norms of the occupation being criminalized. Thus, questions involving the sociology of law are one area where the concept of normative congruity has promising research possibilities.

Proposition Two: The *epidemiology* of occupational crime will be directly related to the extent of worker support for deviant behavior for organizational, occupational and/or work group norms which are in conflict with society's legal standards.

The almost daily record of bribery and payoff confessions to the S.E.C. indicates that this form of behavior has had widespread normative support among practitioners in international sales. Thus, measuring the extent of informal consensus for illegal behaviors in the various normative systems is a possible area to be explored in assessing the amount and distribution of occupational criminality.

Proposition Three: We expect that as the extent of normative support for occupational crime increases that organizational, occupational, and work group variables will take on increasing importance as *explanatory factors* of this phenomenon.

As a result of the "Lockheed scandal" we found that corporate bribery was standard operating procedure in the aerospace industry. This indicates that since the behavior in question is consistent with the normative structure of the workplace, the explained variance of those variables which are related to the nature of work should increase dramatically. We expect that future studies of occupational deviance and crime will base their causal hypotheses on variables such as: organizational formalization, occupational and professional affinity, or notions of "distributive justice" in the work group.

As has become apparent, the purpose of our discussion has been to suggest some testable propositions derivable from the concept, normative incongruity, upon which we can base future studies of occupational deviance and crime. It is our opinion that if we are to systematically understand this phenomenon, we must comprehend the interrelationships between the normative structure of society, the formal work organization, the occupational association, and the work group. It is here where academic energies should be focused to yield that much needed integration of theory and research which to date has plagued this area of inquiry.

METHODOLOGICAL CONSIDERATIONS

No amount of conceptual posturing, derivation of propositions, or even specific suggestions of research directions will magically result in empirically grounded theory and policy-relevant conclusions. To do more than perpetuate the tradition of "much-talk-and-little-action," we must indulge in the laborious, yet central, work of our profession; that is, we must engage in a great variety and volume of empirical studies of occupational deviance and crime.

To date we seem to have gleaned no more understanding from this major arena for deviant social behavior in our industrial society than we have about organized crime, which "everybody knows" is next to impossible to study (Geis and Meier, 1977; Quinney, 1975). Wheeler (1976) has recently provided some insights into why our attention has remained riveted to the study of "nuts and sluts and preverts" (Liazos, 1972) rather than having shifted to include the study of the "legitimate rackets" as developments in our society might suggest.

Frankly, we are a little more optimistic than Wheeler in our prediction of increased emphasis in the near future on occupational crime in criminology. At the same time, we share a deep concern with some others about the *quality* of our anticipated contributions. In other words, we expect there to be a significant increase in the attention given to a wide range of deviations and crimes associated with the world of legitimate work. Without an explicit renewal of our commitment to a value-free scientific method and to an open and courageous consideration of the consequences of our research, we appear to be headed once again toward an eventual major disillusionment with our methods and theory. But, first the good news!

Our discipline's dogged attention to ordinary crime may not, in retrospect, have been all that sterile and stagnant, vis à vis occupational crime. After all, through the study of "labellers" (Lemert, 1972; Schur, 1971; Finestone, 1976), the study of "victims" (Schafer, 1968), the study of "reaction mechanisms," the study of "deterrence" (Morris and Zimring, 1969; Andenaes, 1968) *albeit* largely related to street crime, we have at least gained some sophistication in the use of such concepts as "an organizational system" (Cressey, 1972), "criminalization and de-criminalization" (Dobrovin, 1970), "community-based corrections," "differential vulnerability to labelling," etc. Further, some developments are evident in the methods devised and adopted to study deviance and crime. Also, our efforts to evaluate the impact of prevention and treatment programs have demanded greater clarity and exactness in the measurement of program intent, operations, and consequences. Concomitantly, some progress has been made, at least descriptively, in developing methods to manage the flow of persons, reactions, definitions, and other variables throughout a system of organizations which, collectively, attend society's handling of its deviants. These are just hurried examples which serve as the basis of our relatively optimistic prognosis that we are passing through a threshold of a genuine progress in our understanding of deviance and ordinary crime which is relevant to the study of occupational crime. In sum, in comparison with the past several decades, we are better equipped with concepts, methods, and field research experience to accomplish what needs to be accomplished immediately.

Contrariwise, there appears to be ample reason to doubt whether we will do a good job of it. Because we expend greater efforts, launch a greater number of papers and books, and rearrange our rhetoric to reflect our expanded interests, we are not assured of useful and lasting contributions to our discipline and society. By specifying a limited number of our concerns (and we suspect, your concerns) perhaps we can encourage and strengthen the continued debate about our professional motivations, competence, and impact, and increase the probabilities of quality contributions in the next few years.

To the extent that the subfield of occupational crime and its derivatives become salient to criminology, it will be plagued by some serious problems. Without attention to them and their substantial solution, significant expansion of our knowledge can hardly be expected.

Wheeler touched on our *first* major concern when he wrote:

> Except for a handful of sociologists related to business schools, another handful in other professional schools, and a third group, disparate and of unknown size, who come from wealth or who travel in circles that bring one close to corporate power and authority, we are typically far removed ... ecologically, organizationally, and ideologically, from settings that would make it easy for us to learn more about such activities. [Wheeler, 1976:530]

In a nutshell, few if any of us have the *basic education and/or experience* in industry, commerce, and government at this moment to ask insightful questions, to operationalize concepts intelligently, to access the most fruitful data, to analyze sensitively and to report understandable and useful findings. But let's not be totally discouraged by all this. Through close association with our subjects in the past, i.e., the prostitutes, the hoboes, the junkies, the criminal fence, the juvenile gang member, the felon, the con-man, the pickpocket, the police officer, the parole officer, etc., we have become knowledgeable about ordinary crime. We cannot be expected to have expert knowledge of all social phenomena. Most importantly, after all, we do have a useful perspective, a rigorous methodology, and a commitment to objective analysis which only we can bring to bear on substantive issues. The question, then, is less of *whether* we can become acquainted with our chosen subject matter and more of *how* it will be done. Our guiding principle is that: a linear relationship exists between the extent of prior knowledge of a research subject matter in its natural environment and the sophistication of research efforts constructed to study it.

As a result of our relative ignorance about major segments of the world of work, we conclude that with the exception of a few, most of our efforts will be relatively low level in both theory and research design in the next few years. Much like the situation not long ago in regard to the role of law in criminology, until we make the necessary adjustments toward extensive education and field experience in business, labor, and relevant areas of law and government, our subdiscipline will be severely hampered in its quest for useful, well-informed social analyses of occupational deviance and crime. Interdisciplinary training programs provide a variety of opportunities to address the above problem. Perhaps even more immediate relief can be realized through the mechanism of interdisciplinary research and consultant cooperation with those who are knowledgeable in areas into which our research interests take us. Of particular importance are the areas of business and administrative law, business and society, industrial relations, business economics, accounting, management information systems, and finance. Of course, the uniqueness of local situations must be considered in the construction of training programs' research teams or consultant lists. Interdisciplinary research efforts have always been appealing but very chancy; yet they present possibilities for at least a tentative solution to our problem of gathering expertise in the interdisciplinary character of crime in the work world.

One other pragmatic aside becomes apparent. To assume a major commitment to this area of research entails a major investment of time and perhaps expense. Individually we must carefully consider the viability of research programs in terms of benefits to the discipline, the researchers, the researched, and the funding sources in a reasonable period of time.

Even though conditions are more conducive than ever for research of occupational deviance and crime, we are hesitant to conclude that significant contributions will be immediately forthcoming. If we are not intellectually prepared and practically experienced to a far greater degree than we now are, certainly our contributions will be modest and perhaps counterproductive.

A *second* major unknown intervenes between our readiness to explore a major new area of deviance and our professional ability to do so. It is related to our first reservation but sufficiently distinguished to justify separate treatment. In addition to our basic lack of formal knowledge and personal experience with the subject matter, our *research methods* appear to be embarassingly inadequate to handle the organizational complexities in which occupational crime is embedded with the rigor to which we are accustomed. However, we are not convinced that in our attempts to understand occupational deviance and crime that we can afford to be any less systematic and rigorous, than we have been in the study of juvenile delinquency, murder, or narcotic offenses. To do this well, we must continually remind ourselves of the fundamental requirements of concise conceptual development, appropriate operationalization, validity and reliability testing, and stringent analysis. What must be avoided at all cost (and herein lies the danger) is the conversion of our frustrations into research methodology. That is, our immediate inability to meet adequately the basic requisites of rigorous and appropriate research should not become accepted standard methods of inquiry in this substantive domain.

On the contrary, attempts to satisfy the basic tenets of social science research and policy study should generate a favorable climate for creativity in our methods. In our opinion, there has seldom been a situation more conducive to the development of research procedures, data analysis, and research utilization than now exists in the area of occupational deviance and crime. The scope and context of the substantive concern is immense; the units of analysis and the diversity of data are only vaguely understood by us; the demand for knowledge about such matters is impressive.

More specifically, one of our serious limitations in the study of occupational deviance and crime is our inability to use an occupation or the organization in which it is located as the unit of analysis. Those who have attempted to do so have undoubtedly experienced the frustrations of working with N-sensitive statistics, the reservations about using a highly select piece of data by which to characterize a whole organization, the bewilderment of choosing several appropriate indicators of normative occupational practice when none is correlated with any other, or the disappointment of not being able to gain access to theoretically important data.

Does this mean that as social scientists we are essentially reduced to single-case sociological journalism? We think not. While small, insightful descriptive analyses are frequently useful as generators of initial propositions, heavy reliance on them has not and will not result in a secure grasp of occupational deviance and crime. Analytical units, other than individuals, will likely become more important as practical research experience with occupational deviance and crime will soon reveal.

Wrestling with a research design which will adequately handle theoretically interesting notions will soon carry us beyond individuals and into data sets such as volume of business transactions, bidding and contract awards, marketing and advertising programs, auditing and other internal control mechanisms, labor-management relations, interlocking financial-administrative-ownership arrangements, corporate-government relations, codes of ethics and regulations, safety and health programs, or equal opportunity hiring practices. These are but a few of the rich resources which will likely be tapped in our pursuit of knowledge in our chosen area of deviance and crime in the work world. They also present a challenge, in fact the necessity, for the development of innovative, yet *rigorous,* methods to handle the data adroitly and in a manner which permits replication.

We should not close this very brief discussion of methodological concerns without explicitly reminding ourselves of the need for the meticulous observation of the protection of human subjects and confidentiality requirements. We repeat that our stress on these issues here in no way suggests their greater importance in this area than in any other field. however, our substantive area of concern is relatively new, the topics are notably timely and exciting, organizations and occupations are perhaps more difficult with which to empathize personally and the researcher may feel that all professional standards of confidentiality have been satisfied when official permission to conduct research has been acquired. For these, and probably other, reasons, established procedures to protect research subjects who may directly or indirectly be harmed may not be evident. Perhaps it should be stressed that ethical and human protection matters are particularly acute when dealing in a relatively uncharted area (e.g., deviance in work organizations), in that the indirect effects of the violation of confidentiality or a misleading piece of research are unknown or at least very difficult to suppose beforehand. Assuming the rational model of organizational behavior, one can envision bizarre effects from naive sociology successfully translated into organizational action.

Ethical Considerations. Following hard on the heels of our brief discussion of the critical need for a rigorous approach to knowledge development is our last and perhaps most important point. In spite of the promising conditions for the study of deviance and crime in the world of work, there is yet another pitfall to which others have referred and we believe ought to be made forcefully explicit. We cannot be truly concerned about the major tenets and practices of our respective professions without also being equally concerned about the interplay between the society in which we live and the knowledge we purport to have.

It is almost trite in these times to point out that we social scientists have neglected systematic attention to the social consequences of what we do. In other terms, most of our concern has been focused upon how to approach data, gather it, analyze it, and turn it into scholarly findings. Less importance has been assigned to questioning the source of our scholarly concerns, the selection of our financial patrons and the utilizers of our products. In no way do we propose to thwart the free and open pursuit of knowledge; however, as scholar-citizens we are obligated to address the social reality of knowledge. One has only to look at the various bandwagons in the parade of juvenile delinquency research (Platt, 1969; Finestone, 1976) to develop a self-critical perspective which asks such questions as: Why is this research area so appealing now? What are our motives for doing this? For whom are we working? Who will benefit from this research? Who may be harmed as a result of the research? Why are we not doing something else?

We need not accept uncritically nor feel morally bound to assume a social problem perspective on work-related crime. Even though this issue is more controversial here than adopting a value-free stance toward the study of prostitution, much of what has been written on white-collar crime has revealed a strong and gratuitous condemnation of the perpetrators by its authors. Certainly the popular authors, a la Ralph Nader, leave no doubt of their moral stance. As mentioned as an example above, it seems that scientific enthusiasm accompanied the scholarly support for the creation of juvenile delinquency laws and juvenile courts, though we seemed to have reversed our stand on this issue recently and are just as enthusiastically supporting another perspective. To press the point further, the social problem perspective shows signs of having spawned a social movement within the deviance community. Reform movements strongly supported by academics of various sorts call for greater critical attention to corporate, organized labor, and government misbehavior. Nonobservation of administrative regulations and the relative immunity of some to criminal prosecution is very palatable grist for the reform-minded scholars' mill.

In sum, cries for decriminalization of some behavior seem to be intermingled with cries for greater criminalization, though they are not necessarily seen as intellectually related. Such pursuits by interest groups are not necessarily startling to criminologists, but as scientists and professionals we should be thoughtful about our own participation in the chorus. Given the state of our knowledge about crime and work (especially among corporate operations), on what ground other than personal do we stand? Given the plethora of administrative regulations now and the suspected state of their enforcement, on what ground should we recommend greater regulation or deregulation? Is it possible for us to remain essentially value-free in much of what we do in this area and to be explicit about our values in the remainder? Most of these questions probably have no satisfactory answers, but not to keep them "up front" when research questions are being posed, when projects are being pursued, and when results are being reported is unwise.

Our brief tour de force has been constructed to reorient some empirical studies of deviance and crime associated with work. We have attempted to provide some feasible research suggestions. We have also revealed some considerable concern about both methodological and ethical issues which, if not properly resolved, may significantly constrain the scholarly and practical utility of our forthcoming research. We are cautiously optimistic.

REFERENCES

ANDENAES, J. (1968). "Does punishment deter crime?" Criminal Law Quarterly, 11:76-93.

BENSMAN, J. and GERVER, I. (1963). "Crime and punishment in the factory: The function of deviancy in maintaining the social system." American Sociological Review, 28(August):588-598.

CHAMBLISS, W.J., and SEIDMAN, R.B. (1971). "Law, order and power. Reading, Mass.: Addison-Wesley.

CRESSEY, D.R. (1972). Criminal organization. New York: Harper.

DOBROVIN, W.A. (1970). "The problem of 'overcriminalization'." In J.S. Campbell et al. (eds.), Law and order reconsidered. New York: Bantam Books.

FINESTONE, H. (1976). Victims of change. Westport, Conn.: Greenwood Press.

GEIS, G. (1967). "The heavy electrical equipment antitrust cases of 1961." Pp. 139-151 in M.B. Clinard and R. Quinney (eds.), Criminal behavior systems: A typology. New York: Holt, Rinehart and Winston.

GEIS, G., and MEIER, R. (1977). White-collar crime: Offenses in business, politics and the professions. New York: Free Press.

HORNING, D.N.M. (1970). "Blue collar theft: Conceptions of property, attitudes toward pilfering, and work group norms in a modern industrial plant." Pp. 46-64 in E.O. Smigel and H. Ross (eds.), Crimes against bureaucracy. New York: Van Nostrand Reinhold.

LEMERT, E.M. (1972). Human deviance, social problems, and social control. Englewood Cliffs, N.J.: Prentice-Hall.

LIAZOS, A. (1972). "The poverty of the sociology of deviance: Nuts, sluts and preverts." Social Problems, 20(Summer):103-120.

MORRIS, N., and ZIMRING, F. (1969). "Deterrence and corrections." Annas, 381:137-146.

PLATT, A. (1969). The child savers. Chicago: University of Chicago Press.

QUINNEY, R. (1964). "The study of white collar crime: Toward a reorientation in theory and research." Journal of Criminal Law, Criminology and Police Science, 55(June):208-214.

——— (1970). The social reality of crime. Boston: Little, Brown.

——— (1975). Criminology: Analysis and critique of crime in America. Boston: Little, Brown.

ROBIN, G. (1967). "The corporate and judicial dispositions of employee thieves." Wisconsin Law Review, 685.

ROETHLISBERGER, F., and DICKSON, W.J. (1939). Management and the worker. Cambridge, Mass.: Harvard University Press.

SCHAFER, S. (1968). The victim and his criminal. New York: Random House.

SCHUR, E.M. (1971). Labeling deviant behavior. New York: Harper.

SELLIN, T. (1938). Culture conflict and crime. New York: Social Science Research Council, Bulletin No. 41.

SMITH, R.A. (1961). "The incredible electric conspiracy." Fortune, 63(April): 132-137 and 63(May):161-164. (Reprinted in M. Wolfgang, The sociology of crime and delinquency.)

SUTHERLAND, E.H. (1940). "White collar criminality." American Sociological Review, 5(February):1-12.

——— (1949). White collar crime. New York: Dryden.

TAPPAN, P.W. (1947). "Who is the criminal?" American Sociological Review, 12(February):96-102.

WHEELER, S. (1976). "Trends and problems in the sociological study of crime." Social Problems, 23(June):525-534.

ABOUT THE AUTHORS

JOHN P. CLARK is a Professor in the Department of Sociology, University of Minnesota. He has taught and conducted extensive research in the areas of crime and delinquency, social control organizations, and youth while at the University of Illinois and Minnesota. As a Senior Fulbright Research Scholar in Japan, he developed his current interest in the role of organizations and occupations in deviant behavior.

TOBY DICKMAN is a student of law at the Temple University School of Law. His research interests are in psychology and the biological aspects of crime.

JAMES GAROFALO, a doctoral candidate in criminal justice at the State University of New York (Albany), is currently a research project director at the Criminal Justice Research Center in Albany. His publications include several research monographs in the areas of victim surveys and public attitudes about crime, and he is coauthor (with Michael Hindelang and Michael Gottfredson) of a forthcoming book, *Victims of Personal Crime: An Empirical Foundation for a Theory of Personal Victimization.*

LEONARD J. HIPPCHEN, Ph.D., is an Associate Professor in the Department of Administration of Justice and Public Safety at Virginia Commonwealth University. He was formerly director of criminal justice programs at Glassboro State College and Stephen F. Austin State University and served on the faculty of Florida State University's criminology department. His two most recent books are *The Ecological-Biochemical Approaches to Treatment of Delinquents and Criminals* (forthcoming) and *Handbook on Correctional Classification: Programming for Treatment and Reintegration* (1977).

RICHARD HOLLINGER is a doctoral candidate in sociology at the University of Minnesota. He is presently involved in the collection and analysis of data for his dissertation entitled, "Employee Deviance: Acts Against the Formal Work Organization." His research interests include white-collar crime, deviant behavior, and criminology.

JOAN McCORD is a Professor of Sociology at Drexel University. She is the author of many articles which have appeared in *American Psychologist, Quarterly Journal of Studies on Alcohol, Annals of the New York Academy of Science, Child Development,* and the *Journal of Abnormal and Social Psychology.*

ROBERT F. MEIER is an Assistant Professor in the Program in Social Ecology at the University of California, Irvine. His interests are in the processes of deviance and social control. He is coeditor, with Gilbert Geis, of *White-Collar Crime* (1977) and coauthor, with Marshall B. Clinard, of *Sociology of Deviant Behavior* (forthcoming). He has published in the *American Sociological Review* and the *Journal of Criminal Law and Criminology.*

RAYMOND J. MICHALOWSKI received a Ph.D. in Sociology from Ohio State University in 1973. He has published articles in the area of traffic accident research, corrections, criminal justice education, criminological theory, and critical criminology. He is presently an Associate Professor of Sociology at the University of North Carolina at Charlotte.

W. WILLIAM MINOR, currently an Assistant Professor in the Institute of Criminal Justice and Criminology at the University of Maryland, received his Ph.D. in Criminology at Florida State University in 1975. Previous publications have been in the areas of skyjacking and political crime. Research interests for the immediate future include neutralization theory and a study of arson.

HAROLD E. PEPINSKY, author of *Crime and Conflict* (1976), is Associate Professor of Foreign Studies and East Asian Languages and Cultures at Indiana University, Bloomington.

LEONARD SAVITZ, Professor of Sociology at Temple University, has published and done research in the areas of urban life and delinquency, fear of crime, gang behavior, and drugs.

STANLEY H. TURNER is an Associate Professor of Sociology at Temple University. His research interests are the measurement of crime and the activities of the prosecutor.